SUCCESSFUL LIFE SKILLS FOR TEENS

MASTER SELF-CONFIDENCE, EMOTIONAL
INTELLIGENCE, EFFECTIVE TIME
MANAGEMENT & COMMUNICATION, BUILD
SOCIAL SKILLS, & STRENGTHEN MENTAL
HEALTH FOR A BETTER FUTURE!

CHAD K. SMITH, MBA

GROWTH MINDSET PUBLISHING

CONTENTS

INTRODUCTION

"Your life does not get better by chance, it gets better by change."

— JIM ROHN

How do you feel about presentations? For most teenagers, they're the stuff nightmares are made of, and they cause anxiety for weeks before they happen. My friend's son James used to be that way. I remember hanging out at their house one weekend while he was getting ready for a big presentation, and you could almost feel the nerves coming off him. He was purely prepared for this presentation, but his emotions and thoughts were plagued by self-doubt and terror about speaking in public. It's a different story now. I've seen him deliver speeches so confidently that it's impossible to imagine him ever having been nervous. So, what sparked the change? Given the book you're reading, it probably won't surprise you to hear that it was learning some essential life skills that helped him manage his emotions and raise his confidence.

This book is your life-changing guide to unlocking those very same skills. You are already motivated because you are reading it right now and I am very proud of you! My goal is to empower you with the tools you need to build unshakeable self-confidence, enhance your emotional intelligence, master time management, and make strong social connections. These skills are the keys to reaching your fullest potential, and they'll help you to turn everyday challenges into opportunities for growth and success.

The teenage years are tough. I remember them all too well. It felt like every day meant facing a new battle. For me, it wasn't public speaking that was the issue. I had issues controlling my emotions and I unintentionally let them get the best of me. We all have our unique circumstances, but perhaps yours is managing your time or maybe it's planning for the future. Or maybe you feel like *everything's* worrying you. No matter what you're struggling with, this book will help you.

We will be focusing on real world situations and giving you interactive exercises that keep you actively involved. Throughout this book, you will dive into hands-on activities designed to help you practice, reflect, and truly build the skills you are learning. By the time you finish this book, you will be ready to take on any challenge life throws at you. You will have new foundations, essential skills, real experience, and the confidence to crush whatever comes your way! I want you to engage and implement these lessons in your everyday life as you go along through this book, that's how you'll really get a chance to feel the benefits of moving forward in life with unstoppable confidence!

"What benefits?" you might be asking. How about a big boost in self-confidence and feeling ready to welcome new challenges? Or a keen emotional awareness that means you can understand and manage your feelings more effectively? Those are big ones on their own, but you'll also equip yourself with the skills you need to become a time management master with the ability to balance your schoolwork, hobbies, and social life. You'll discover the secret to strengthening your social connections, too, and I'm sure you'll quickly start to see improvements in your relationships with friends, family, and even acquaintances you meet.

Mastering these life skills is going to help you survive these tough teenage years with minimal stress, but it's also going to give you the boost you need to thrive and prepare for a successful adulthood. Did you know that employers actually think these skills are more important to career advancement than the technical skills people need to do their specific jobs? 94% of executives feel this way, and what this should tell you is that you're going to need these skills not just to do well in your personal life, but to excel in your career too. If that sounds far-fetched to you, think of it this way: These are the skills that will make you more resilient and adaptable when you're faced with change, and that's something that's very important in the professional world, no matter what field you work.

This is a subject I know quite well. As a retired United States Marine and a dedicated personal finance author, I have spent most of my life witnessing the power of discipline and resilience. I developed these traits early on, and they have shaped my life and career deeply. What has struck me even more is seeing these qualities grow in others I've mentored and the full impact they have on life. I am not exaggerating when I say the change is truly transformative. I have seen young people join the Marines with more enthusiasm, and through training, they become confident, ambitious, and proactive. My goal is to provide you with all the tools necessary to take control of your life, find the right fit for your passions, and create a future you are excited to tackle, no matter what that future holds.

Before we begin, please take a moment to read and take action. Don't just absorb the words—think about how they can help you grow and shape a stronger mindset. As you read, I encourage you to keep a journal or a fresh notebook to write down your thoughts along the way. This will make your journey much more impactful because putting your thoughts, plans, and lessons into writing turns ideas into real progress. By the time you finish this book, you will have gained powerful skills and a deeper understanding of your true potential. My goal is for you to embrace these lessons, write out your plans, and use them to create the life you want.

So, are you ready? Then let's get to work!

CHAPTER 1
BUILDING SELF-CONFIDENCE

"You have to believe in yourself when no one else does."

— SERENA WILLIAMS

I introduced you to my friend's son James in the introduction. When I told him I was writing this book, I asked him if he would put me in touch with some of his friends so that I could hear their stories. I wasn't disappointed—between them, they gave me an example for pretty much everything I wanted to cover in the book. We'll start with Mia.

Mia loved art, and James says she's always been very talented, yet she was always hesitant to share her paintings with her class. Even though on one level, she knew she was skilled at it, she couldn't shake the self-doubt. She told me it was almost like there was a voice inside her constantly whispering that her work wasn't good enough. She worked on one project for weeks, refusing to let anyone see it because she was so unsure of herself. But when she finally revealed her piece, her classmates and teacher literally applauded. They could see her unique vision and talent, and it prompted a reaction Mia could never have imagined. This was the confidence she needed, and it completely transformed how she viewed herself. When I interviewed her, she was happy to show me her work, and she laughed about how shy she'd been to share it in the past.

Mia has a spark, and this chapter is all about helping you discover yours. Building self-confidence is not just about standing tall or speaking loudly. It is about understanding your worth and valuing yourself without needing constant validation from others, and this is where we will begin our exploration.

Understanding Your Self-Worth

You know how a house needs a strong foundation before anything else can be built? Your self-confidence works the same way. You cannot build it until you understand your own worth, first. Self-worth is your inner value, the beliefs you hold about yourself deep down. It is not about what others think of you or how many likes you receive from your latest post. That stuff does not matter at all. It's about recognizing that you're valuable simply because you exist. That's not the same thing as self-esteem. Self-esteem is how you feel about yourself in different situations. While self-worth stays steady, self-esteem can fluctuate based on external factors.

Think about how you feel when someone compliments your outfit or praises your performance. That's external validation, and it created a great feeling, but it's not something you can rely on. It would be like neglecting to build that foundation we talked about and building your house directly onto sand: It's going to be unstable, and it isn't going to last very long. This is where internal validation comes into play. This means acknowledging your worth, regardless of what anyone else thinks. I know it isn't always easy, but it means saying to yourself, "I have value," even when it seems like the rest of the world feels otherwise.

To truly understand self-worth, take a moment to identify the things that make you unique. What are your strengths? What do you value? If you spend some time reflecting on these questions, you will begin to form a clearer sense of who you are. It might help to keep a journal where you jot down things you are proud of or values that matter to you. Another powerful practice is to look at yourself in the mirror and say, "I like myself." Do not stop until you genuinely believe it. Over time, this practice can boost your confidence and keep your strengths fresh in your mind, reminding you who you are at your best—even during challenging moments filled with self-doubt.

Reflective Journaling Exercise

Grab a notebook, and set aside time each week to write about what makes you unique. Include moments that made you feel proud or the values you've noticed guiding your actions.

Challenging Negative Beliefs

Even the most confident person is sometimes challenged by negative thoughts that tell them they're not good enough or smart enough, so if this is something you struggle with, don't worry because you're in good company. Here's the thing, though: You can challenge and change them, and this is the secret that helps those confident people move past the moment.

The first thing to do is notice when these thoughts arise. When you catch one, ask yourself if it's based on facts or assumptions. Often, negative thoughts are just stories we tell ourselves, and they're not really based in reality. Let me give you an example.

Before James' newfound confidence, he told me that he'd never be good at public speaking because he wasn't that interesting. "Are you sure?" I asked him. "What evidence do you have?" It turned out he had none. This was all his perception of himself, and he didn't have a single fact to back it up. Simply realizing this is empowering. Once you've identified the negative thought, try reframing it. Instead of thinking, "I always mess up," say, "I made a mistake this time, but I can learn from it." Instead of thinking, "No one likes me," tell yourself, "I have a lot to offer other people."

This process is called cognitive restructuring. It is like giving your thoughts a makeover by swapping out the negative ones and actively replacing those thoughts with ones that build confidence! It will take some practice, but as you actively think about it, you will start see yourself in a more positive and powerful way.

This ties in with self-acceptance. Self-acceptance means accepting all parts of yourself that are good and the messy. Remember, nobody's perfect and perfection is a myth! A far better course of action is to focus on accepting yourself, flaws and all. This doesn't mean that you can't change those flaws, but you can when you discipline yourself to accept them.

Writing Self-Acceptance Letters

Writing self-acceptance letters can be a powerful way to work through self-doubt or emotional challenges. The idea is to acknowledge the areas where you feel insecure, then counter them with affirmations that highlight your strengths. For example, "I may struggle with math, but I'm creative and resilient," or "I have a hard time speaking in front of a lot of people, but I'm a really good listener." As you can see, "but" is the key word here. For every insecurity you find, add a "but," and challenge yourself to counter it with a positive.

Take a moment now to write a letter to yourself. Begin by expressing your insecurities, but follow them with positive affirmations that highlight your strengths and resilience. Do it now, and you'll have some practice behind you for when you really need it.

If writing doesn't work for you, you could try mindfulness. All this really means is being present in each moment and being gentle with yourself during tough times rather than judging yourself harshly or criticizing yourself for not measuring up (Neff and Germer 2019).

Don't expect any of this to happen overnight, though. Building your self-confidence is a gradual process that involves understanding your worth, challenging your negative thoughts, and embracing who you are wholly and unapologetically. That's a lot to do, and you can't expect to do it all in one go because it takes practice and self-discipline.

The Power of Positive Self-Talk

The alarm goes off early on Monday morning. How do you feel? You might think, "Ugh, I'm so tired. I can't handle this week." That's a classic example of self-talk, the daily dialogue running through your mind. Self-talk influences how you perceive yourself and the world around you, and the scary thing is, you probably don't even hear it a lot of the time. But it can shape your confidence, attitude, and even your actions, so it's worth paying attention (Allen n.d.). When it's negative, it can hold you back by constantly reminding you of your doubts and fears, but when it's positive, it's a powerful tool for building your confidence and resilience. If you're able to change your self-talk from "I can't do this" to "I'll give it my best shot," you can transform your mindset from defeated to determined, and that's a very powerful thing.

Positive self-talk is about building a supportive inner dialogue that reinforces your strengths and capabilities and leaves you feeling optimistic (Richards 2022). It's a bit like having your own personal cheerleader in your head, reminding you of what you can achieve. When you have a daunting task ahead of you—an impending exam or a sports competition, for example—if you have an internal voice saying, "I've prepared well, and I can handle this," it can stop you from feeling so overwhelmed and help you feel prepared to tackle the challenge head-on.

This is all easy to say, but how do you actually do it? Start with daily affirmations. These are simple, positive statements that you repeat to yourself to reinforce your strengths and aspirations so that you feel more confident in yourself (Wisner 2024). They might say, "I am capable of achieving my goals," or "Every day, I grow stronger and more confident." The secret is to be consistent about it. Make it a part of your routine—every morning, as you brush your teeth, for example, or each night before you go to bed.

Positive self-talk is also very motivating. Let's say you're standing at the start line of a marathon (and I don't mean this literally— your marathon could be anything from a big presentation to applying for a job). How you talk to yourself in this situation matters. You don't want to tell yourself that you don't stand a chance because that will automatically set you off with the wrong mindset. You want to tell yourself you're going to succeed. Visualization will help your future in almost everything. Picture yourself achieving your goal. Picture every detail: how you feel, what you see, the sound of applause or congratulations at the end. This creates a mental blueprint that can boost your confidence and motivation (Globokar 2020). You can support this with your self-talk, and to take this to the next level, you might want to try using self-motivation scripts. Really, this just means giving yourself little pep talks that focus on your abilities and determination; the fact that they're "scripts" simply means that you've prepared them. You might, for example, have a script that says, "I am prepared for this moment because I have worked very hard and I know will succeed." Then visualize it happening.

Your own self-talk is powerful, but so is the talk you hear from other people. Ideally, you want to be surrounded by people who lift you rather than drag you down. Supportive social circles can include friends who encourage you or family members who believe in you. If you feel like this is something you're missing right now, seek out nurturing and positive environments—a club at school, perhaps, or an online community that shares your interests.

Bear in mind, too, that what you consume—through reading or media—also impacts your self-talk (Landers 2023). If you choose books or podcasts that inspire and motivate you, it will reinforce your feelings of positivity. Narratives that showcase resilience and triumph can subtly influence your self-talk by showing what's possible when someone believes in themselves. It's a bit like when people say, "You are what you eat," referring to the fact that a healthy diet equates to a healthy body: You are the media you consume. If you soak up positive and inspiring messages, this is going to rub off on you.

Your goal is to make your inner voice one that encourages you rather than criticizes you. You're not aiming just to change your words; your goal is to use those words to change your perceptions and behaviors. The more you practice, the more clearly you'll see how this can help you rise to challenges and pursue your goals confidently. Just do it. Act. Take those steps with confidence because you have practice so hard. You got this!

Overcoming the Fear of Failure

Failure—just the word that can make your stomach churn, can't it? But what if we flipped the script and saw failure not as the end but as a system for success? You may have heard this idea in the context of Thomas Edison, who famously said, "I have not failed. I've just found 10,000 ways that won't work" (Thomas Edison Foundations n.d.). His relentless pursuit led him to patent the electric light bulb, and all because of his willingness to view failure as a teacher rather than a setback (McKelvie and Peterson 2022). You're going to need this kind of mindset shift if you want to overcome the fear of failure. When we redefine failure as an opportunity for growth, we open up a world of possibilities (Phillimore 2024).

If you're wondering how on earth you're meant to do this, the secret is to build your resilience, and that takes practice. Have you ever heard of a "growth mindset?" This is where you want to start. A growth mindset believes that challenges and setbacks are opportunities to learn and grow; it believes that your abilities aren't fixed and you're capable of developing (Cote 2022). To train yourself in this mindset, engage in resilience-building exercises like setting small, achievable goals that stretch your abilities but aren't overwhelming. You want to be challenged, but not so challenged that you become discouraged. When you reach your mini-goals successfully, you'll feel a sense of accomplishment that will fuel further motivation and resilience (Scott n.d.). You'll need to be adaptable, too. Life is always going to throw you curveballs, and you're going to need to be able to pivot and adjust your approach. When you can do this, I'm sure you'll find that you bounce back stronger and more determined.

You can't do all of this from within your comfort zone, however. You're going to need to step outside of it every now and then.

Growth happens when you challenge yourself beyond the familiar (Page 2020). Encourage yourself to take calculated risks. Start with small challenges that push your boundaries but aren't too daunting. I'm talking about something like trying a new hobby or speaking up in class when you usually would not speak. You can gradually increase the difficulty of the challenges as your confidence grows. This gradual exposure will help you build your confidence incrementally and over time, this will make it easier to take larger risks. This is one of the things James did to overcome his fear of public speaking. He started by challenging himself to answer one question in every class he took. That was very hard for him at first, but once it became a habit, it didn't make him anxious anymore, and it paved the way for a huge transformation in his confidence.

Post-Failure Reflection Techniques

If you're to process your failures constructively, you're going to need to reflect on them. Each time you experience a setback, take some time to reflect on what happened and why. You may also want to keep a growth journal to document your thoughts and feelings after each experience. The point isn't to dwell on the negative but to understand the situation better and identify the things you could improve next time. Ask yourself questions like, "What can I learn from this experience?" or "How can I approach this differently next time?" To motivate yourself to do this when the time comes, create a list of questions to guide your reflection now.

We like to talk about "bouncing back," but embracing failure as a natural part of life is more about bouncing *forward* with newfound resilience, insights, and strategies to handle it better. When you redefine failure as a purpose rather than a roadblock, you can empower yourself to take risks and pursue your dreams, no matter what. Remember that every successful person has faced failure at some point. Their secret was not to let it stop them and, instead, learn from the experience. There will be moments when everything feels heavy. Your mind will be tested, your body exhausted, and quitting might seem like an easy way out. But don't do it. Success is not easy so never fall for that trap! Your breakthrough often comes right after the moment where you almost gave up. Keep going because you're closer than you think.

Search online and you will find stories with the same type of encouragement. Walt Disney was once fired from a newspaper for "lacking imagination," yet he went on to build an entertainment empire that still inspires people today (Bright Side n.d.). His journey, along with stories like Steve Jobs returning to Apple after being pushed out, shows how persistence and adaptability can turn setbacks into powerful comebacks (Walker n.d.). Failure is just one chapter in your future success story, fueling your mind with motivation and pushing you closer to outcomes newspapers will write about!

Celebrating Small Wins

Did you know that you accomplish something every day? Sometimes you might ace a quiz, maybe you help a friend, or perhaps you make it all the way through your to-do list. On other days, maybe your greatest achievement is getting out of bed because you don't have the energy to move. These might seem like small things, but they're wins worth celebrating—even getting out of bed on a hard day. Recognizing your small achievements will help you keep up the momentum and build the confidence you need in order to tackle bigger challenges. If you make a point of acknowledging these victories, you'll create a positive feedback loop where success breeds more success (McNally 2024).

A simple way to do this is to keep a daily achievement log. At the end of each day, jot down at least three things you accomplished. It could be anything from finishing your homework on time to trying a new hobby. No matter how defeated you feel that day, you'll have a tangible reminder of your capabilities and growth, and this will help you build your resilience.

Milestones, no matter how small, deserve acknowledgment, and when you meet them, it's important to take a moment to celebrate. Perhaps you give yourself a small treat or an extra half-hour doing something you love. It will boost your morale and reinforce the habit of setting and achieving goals (McNally 2024).

In Chapter Eight, we're going to talk about goal setting. Integrating rewards with your goals will help you to maintain your focus and motivation (Thomas n.d.). For instance, if your goal is to run a mile without stopping, perhaps each quarter-mile improvement earns you a reward. Your reward should be personal to you and what will motivate you. Perhaps you reward yourself with a night out with friends or a new book you've been eyeing. Whatever you choose, your reward should feel meaningful and encourage you to keep pushing forward.

Celebrating small wins helps build a cycle of positive reinforcement that boosts both your confidence and motivation (McNally 2025). As we mentioned earlier, visualizing your progress and future success keeps that momentum going. One powerful way to do this is by creating a vision board. A vision board displays your goals and achievements, giving you daily motivation every time you see it. Simply gather images and words that represent what you're aiming for, then arrange them on a large piece of card. Place it somewhere visible so you see it every day to keep your goals fresh in your mind. Each image or phrase becomes a reminder of how far you've come and what you're still working to achieve (Clancy 2025).

Reflection is important in all areas of personal growth, and in this case, it's a powerful motivator (Pavlou 2024). Every now and then, make an effort to look back at where you started compared to where you are now. You'll see how far you've come, and this will strengthen your belief in your path. It's easy to forget your past achievements when you're busy focusing on future goals, but remembering those steps will reinforce your ability to succeed.

If you don't feel like you're having any issues with your confidence right now, you might be inclined to brush over some of these things. But we're not just talking about boosting your confidence today, we're talking about building a foundation for long-term success and happiness. Celebrating your small wins will build your resilience and perseverance, and you'll develop an attitude of gratitude and positivity that will carry you through every challenge and triumph that lies ahead of you.

No matter how confident you are sometimes emotions take over and make it hard to stay positive. Don't worry, though because there are strategies you can use to help you manage your emotions, too. You'll find out all about them in the next chapter.

CHAPTER 2
MASTERING EMOTIONAL INTELLIGENCE

"The greatest gift that you can give to others is the gift of unconditional love and acceptance."

— BRIAN TRACY

E motional intelligence sounds a bit intimidating at first, but it simply refers to having the ability to understand, interpret, show, and control emotions. It's important for navigating your own emotional landscape, but it's also about having the ability to read and respond to emotions in other people, so it's important in a social context (Cherry 2024). It's arguably one of the most important life skills you can learn, and it will be our focus in this chapter.

Recognizing and Naming Emotions

You know that feeling when you're scrolling through your phone, and suddenly something gets to you? Maybe it's a friend's post or a random meme, and you find yourself feeling something intense.

But what exactly is that feeling? Is it annoyance, jealousy, or excitement? Sometimes it's hard to know when it takes you by surprise like this, and this is why it's important to be able to recognize and name your emotions. When you can pinpoint what you're feeling, you have control over how you react. This is the heart of emotional awareness, and this is a big part of emotional intelligence. It's not just about knowing that you're upset (although that's part of it), it's also about understanding *why* you're upset. When you understand the reason, it's easier to respond more thoughtfully rather than impulsively, and this is very good for your relationships (Adams 2025).

Your emotional vocabulary is made up of the words you use to describe your emotions. I'm sure you remember teachers trying to encourage you to use words like "frustrated," or "anxious" when you were younger. They were trying to encourage you to go beyond just "happy" or "sad" and expand your emotional vocabulary. If you think yours could still do with some work, an emotion wheel might help you here. It's like a color wheel, but for feelings, and it will help you identify nuances in your emotions. You can find plenty online, and if it will help you to articulate your feelings, it's definitely going to be worth it because it will mean that you're better equipped to handle them (Poyner 2024).

If you're not used to paying attention to your emotions, keeping an emotion journal will help you here. Every day, jot down what you felt at different points and what triggered those feelings. Over time, you'll start to see patterns. You might notice that certain days or events trigger specific emotions, for example, and many people find that this awareness helps them to manage their reactions better. You might even want to download a daily mood tracking chart so you can visualize the patterns more clearly.

We touched on mindfulness briefly earlier on, and this is another powerful tool for recognizing your emotions. Mindfulness encourages you to be present and acknowledge your feelings without judgment. If you're new to mindfulness, you might feel a bit lost right now, but don't worry—it's really very simple, and breathing exercises can help you get started. Try taking deep breaths when you notice intense emotions rising up inside you. This will give you a moment to pause and identify what you're experiencing. That's going to be difficult to do in the heat of the moment unless you've practiced it, though, so I'd recommend using mindful meditation practices to help you develop your awareness. By spending a few minutes each day in stillness, focusing on your breath, you'll train yourself to notice your emotions as they arise (Francis 2020). You can do this simply by focusing your mind and concentrating on your breathing, but if you feel you'd like a little more guidance to begin with, there are plenty of free meditations online.

The connection between our emotions and our actions is significant. Our emotions often drive our actions, sometimes without us even realizing it, and when we understand this, we can control our reactions better. Imagine a situation where someone bumps into you in the corridor. Your initial emotion might be anger, and this might lead you to impulsive reactions like shouting or making rude gestures. But if you recognize your anger, you can choose a different action, like taking a deep breath or walking away.

The best way to prepare for this is to practice cause-and-effect scenarios—a bit like you would in a role-playing exercise. It will allow you to explore different emotional responses in a controlled setting. For example, if someone teases you at school, how does that make you feel? What are your initial reactions? If you reflect on previous scenarios like this, you should start to see how your emotions influence your actions and how alternative responses could lead to different outcomes.

Emotion Journal

Spend a week recording your emotions in a journal. Note the specific emotion, what triggered it, and how you reacted. Use this information to identify patterns and consider alternative responses for the future.

Managing Stress and Anxiety

Life is anything but straightforward. One minute, you're fine, and the next, it feels like everything's piling up on top of you, and it's overwhelming. How can you manage this chaos? It's simple, really: You have to identify the stressors.

Stressors are those little (or big) things that trigger your stress response (Wooll 2022). They can range from school deadlines and personal goals to family expectations and social pressures, and being able to recognize them will help you to understand how they're affecting your emotional and physical well-being. Stress inventory worksheets can help you pinpoint these triggers by encouraging you to list everyday stressors and reflect on how they affect you. We'll look at how you can make one of these shortly. You can also keep a personal stress log, much like the emotion journal we just discussed, only focusing on the moments you feel stressed and what triggered that feeling. Again, you'll begin to see patterns emerging, and this will help you to tackle stress more effectively.

If you're thinking that identifying what's stressing you out isn't going to solve the problem, you're right. The next step is coping with these things. You know how having a variety of tools in a toolbox means you're prepared for lots of different situations? That's how coping strategies are, too, and it's best to have as many as possible up your sleeve. I'll introduce you to two of my favorites now, and, conveniently, they're the easiest to use no matter where you are.

We'll start with guided imagery, which is a relaxation technique that encourages you to focus on positive feelings (West 2022). The idea is to transport yourself to a peaceful place, even if it's just in your mind. Imagine yourself on a serene beach or in a quiet forest, and let that mental image wash over you, calming your nerves. This is really all it takes.

If you want something more physical than this, progressive muscle relaxation might be a good call. Here, the goal is to tense and then relax each muscle group gradually, which helps to reduce the tension in your body. You should ideally be lying down to do this, and you should hold each muscle group tensed for five seconds before you release it. Allow it to relax for at least 10 seconds before starting on the next group (Nunez 2020). Both this and guided imagery can be practiced anywhere (you don't have to lie down if it's not appropriate), and this gives you handy go-to strategies that you can use whenever anxiety strikes.

A lot of teenagers struggle with fitting their coping strategies into their daily life, and this is where creating a stress management plan can help. It'll give you the structure you need while you make these things into habits. You want to consider both daily and long-term strategies. You could set aside 15 minutes a day for mindfulness, for example, which should help to reduce your stress on a daily basis. You might include self-care routines that recharge you, such as reading a book, walking, working out, or spending time with your friends. To make your plan really effective, you'll need to recognize signs of escalating stress and include steps you can take to help you manage it before it becomes overwhelming.

I'd like to remind you at this point that you're not alone. Reach out to friends or family members who can lend an ear or offer advice when you need it. These people genuinely care about your well-being, and they'll be able to give you emotional support and practical help when you need it. If your stress and anxiety start to feel overwhelming, it may be time to seek help from a professional. There is nothing shameful about asking for support when you need it. Reaching out shows strength and self-awareness. Therapists and counselors are trained to offer guidance and coping techniques that take your personal circumstances into account and give you the strategies that will help you the most. Knowing when to ask for help is important to maintaining your emotional health, and it's never a sign of weakness. In fact, it's always a sign of strength.

Stress Inventory Worksheet

I'd like you to take a moment now to work on that stress inventory worksheet we discussed earlier. List all the potential stressors you know sometimes affect you, such as schoolwork, social events, or family issues. On a scale of one to five, rate each one based on how much it affects you, and think about why this is the case. What you're doing here is becoming more emotionally aware, and it will help you to identify when you're feeling stressed in the moment when slowing down and paying attention isn't always easy.

When I talk about managing your stress, I don't mean you should be trying to eliminate it. That's impossible, but you can find ways to cope with it. Identifying your stressors will give you insight into what triggers your stress and anxiety, and this will give you the power to address these issues directly. Meanwhile, you can use your coping strategies to calm your mind and body, which will reduce the grip anxiety has on your day-to-day life.

Practicing Empathy in Everyday Life

Let's step away from ourselves now and into someone else's shoes, seeing the world from their perspective. That's empathy. A lot of people get this confused with sympathy, which is when you feel sorry for someone, but it's actually quite different. Empathy means understanding and sharing their experiences and emotions, even if they differ from yours (Cherry 2024). To put this into context, let's say your friend just lost their dog. Sympathy might make you say, "I'm sorry for your loss," but empathy goes deeper. It involves connecting with their pain because you've experienced something similar or can deeply imagine their feelings. This connection significantly affects your emotional intelligence and helps you to build stronger relationships.

But how do you get better at showing empathy? The good news is that it is a skill you can develop with practice. One powerful way to begin is by practicing perspective taking. This means imagining yourself in someone else's situation and making an effort to understand how they might be feeling and what they could be thinking. Try this with the people around you—your friends, members of your family, and strangers you meet at the bus stop. Take a moment to think about their day, their struggles, and how they might feel. I can almost guarantee that it will stop you in your tracks if you catch yourself about to yell at your mom for forgetting to bring your sneakers when you remember that she had a really stressful thing in her day, and she's probably still processing it.

Think about how this might look in your life right now. Let's say you're struggling with a group project because someone isn't pulling their weight. Instead of jumping to conclusions or reacting with frustration, take a moment to consider their perspective. Could it be that they're overwhelmed by their other responsibilities? Is there something happening in their personal life affecting their contribution? Approaching them with empathy might lead to a more productive and supportive conversation, and at the very least, it will help you understand what's going on for them.

When you use empathy in conversations, you connect with people in a better way. You think about how they feel and where they're coming from, which helps you understand them more. Reflective listening is one way to strengthen your communication skills. What do I mean by this? Basically, I mean going beyond just hearing the words someone says and making an effort to understand the emotions behind them and demonstrate this to them (Herrity 2025). When someone shares something with you, reflect back what you heard to show that you understood. For example, if your friend tells you that they're stressed about exams, you might say, "It sounds like you're feeling overwhelmed by the pressure." Of course, this isn't where the conversation ends—and it isn't meant to be. With that gesture, you've offered compassion and gently opened the way for a deeper connection. You're almost certain to get a thoughtful response that will allow you to connect even more deeply with your friend.

As you can see, responding with empathy in conversations goes beyond just listening. You have to acknowledge the other person's feelings and show genuine concern. If someone shares bad news with you, instead of simply saying, "That sucks," try adding, "I'm sorry to hear that happened. How can I help?" This will help you build trust and connection at the same time.

But empathy doesn't only apply to your individual interactions. It's also really important in understanding diverse perspectives and cultural backgrounds. The world is filled with different cultures and stories. Being empathetic means being open to these differences and seeking to understand them. One simple way to explore cultural stories is by reading books or watching films from around the world. They help you understand different values, challenges, and achievements through powerful storytelling.

This is cultural empathy, and you can deepen yours by making an effort to interact with people from different backgrounds or participating in multicultural events. These experiences will broaden your understanding and appreciation of diversity and teach you that while our backgrounds may differ, our emotions are universally human. It'll also open you up to new perspectives and ideas, and that's always a good thing.

While serving in the military, I had the opportunity to work with people from all over the country and the world, each bringing their own unique accents, favorite foods, family traditions, and ways of life shaped by the places they called home.

Imagine how powerful the world could be if everyone practiced empathy. It has the strength to break down walls, reduce prejudice, and bring people together despite their differences. If we all made empathy part of our daily lives, we'd help build a more compassionate and understanding world.

Empathy doesn't mean you have to agree with everyone or accept every behavior. All you have to do is try to understand where those thoughts and behaviors come from and respond with kindness rather than judgment. The result? Better relationships and improved emotional intelligence. What an incredible life skill to have!

Building empathy is like strengthening a muscle as it takes consistent effort and practice. The more you practice the things we've talked about, the more empathetic you'll become. This growth will benefit your personal life and prepare you for future roles where empathy is crucial—everything from supporting a friend in a time of need to leading a team at work. Empathy teaches us that everyone has a story worth hearing and a perspective worth considering. It's a huge gift and definitely a skill worth practicing.

Active Listening Techniques

Have you ever found yourself sitting in class, determined to listen to your teacher explain a new concept, only to realize you have no idea what they said? You nod along, but your mind is elsewhere, and you suddenly realize you haven't really been paying attention. This is where active listening comes in, and it's key to effective communication and relationship-building, not just for paying attention in class. Active listening means fully concentrating, understanding, and responding to what's being said rather than just hearing the words. In essence, it's about engaging with the speaker.

Active listening requires you to pay attention, show that you're listening, provide feedback, and respond appropriately. We often think we're paying attention, but really, we're just going through the motions. To do it effectively, we need to minimize distractions and focus fully on the speaker, all the time, showing that we're listening through our body language. This doesn't need you to do anything elaborate, just simply make eye contact and nod at the appropriate times to show you're listening. The last part of the equation, providing feedback, involves summarizing or paraphrasing what you've heard to make sure that you've understood correctly (Cuncic 2024).

This is something you can practice in your everyday interactions. To practice paraphrasing, restate what the speaker said in your own words. For instance, if your friend says she's stressed about her exams, you might say, "So, you're feeling overwhelmed with everything coming up?" By doing this, you'll make her feel truly heard and understood. Summarizing does a similar thing. Here, you condense the main points into a brief overview—so in our example, you might say, "The exams are so stressful and it's hard to see how to prepare for them." Reflective responses also help. To practice this, mirror the emotions you sense the person speaking is feeling, so you might say, "It sounds like you're frustrated with this situation."

You can also ask open-ended questions to encourage detailed responses and deeper conversations. Instead of asking yes/no questions, which can quickly shut a conversation down, try to say something like, "What do you think about this?" or "How did that make you feel?" These questions invite the speaker to explore their thoughts and feelings further, and they pave the way for a deeper conversation.

Active listening isn't always easy. It's easy to let distractions and preconceived notions get in the way—and distractions aren't always as obvious as you might think. They can be external, like noise or phones, or they can be internal, like wandering thoughts. These are the ones I personally find the most challenging. To overcome these barriers, you'll need to identify your specific listening obstacles—do you get bored easily? Do you interrupt? Once you're clear which of your habits are getting in the way, you can work on minimizing them.

Minimizing distractions means creating an environment that's conducive to listening. Put your phone away during conversations, and choose quieter places for really important or delicate discussions. Managing your internal distractions can be a little harder, but you can make yourself do it by focusing on the present moment. Practicing mindfulness will really help you to sharpen this focus.

Active listening can benefit everyone in any setting. It's helpful at school, and it's helpful in every one of your personal relationships.

In class discussions or seminars, you need to engage fully with the material and participate actively. Ask questions if you're confused, and contribute thoughtfully whenever you can. In this context, active listening is furthering your learning and making you a valuable member of the group. In your personal relationships, it builds understanding and trust (MacArthur 2024). It shows that you value the other person's perspective, and it can lead you into deeper connected discussions and, as a result, develop a stronger bond.

You're going to need to be adept at active listening in order to navigate difficult conversations effectively. You know the kinds of conversations where emotions run high or opinions clash? Approach them with an open mind and a willingness to understand the other person's point of view. Listen for emotions as carefully as you listen to the words, and respond with empathy.

Every facet of emotional intelligence empowers you to understand yourself and others better, and this will make the social landscape much easier and more rewarding to navigate. In the next chapter, we'll explore this further, looking at other ways in which you can strengthen your social skills.

CHAPTER 3

STRENGTHENING SOCIAL SKILLS

"Life's most persistent and urgent question is, 'What are you doing for others?'"

— DR. MARTIN LUTHER KING, JR.

As you've already seen, there's a strong relationship between emotional intelligence and good social skills. The more you practice the skills we looked at in the last chapter, the easier you'll find it to navigate the social landscape. Nonetheless, there are a few more things we can look at to help you in this area.

Building Healthy Friendships

High school friendships, as I'm sure you know, can either lift you up or drag you down. The key to striking a balance and making sure they make you feel good more often than they make you feel bad is to work on developing healthy friendships. These are the friendships that offer both of you trust, mutual respect, and shared interests.

Trust is the most important part of this equation. You need to know that your secrets are safe and your friend has your back, and your friend needs to know the same about you. Without trust, you're going to find it very difficult to have mutual respect, which means valuing each other's opinions and boundaries, even when they don't align perfectly. Your shared interests, meanwhile, give you common ground on which you can have shared experiences and build memories together. A supportive friend listens without judgment, celebrates your victories, and stands by you in tough times. Friendships flourish when you have similar values and your interests align, although it's important to note that this doesn't mean that you can't also enjoy different things from each other or have different opinions.

But how do you differentiate between healthy and toxic relationships? We'll go over the key signs now. A toxic friendship often involves manipulation, constant negativity, or one-sided efforts. If a friend belittles you, guilt-trips you into doing things, or makes you feel drained rather than uplifted, these are red flags. You shouldn't feel depleted in energy after spending time with a friend, and you shouldn't feel that you have to walk on eggshells around them, but if you do, this is a sign that the friendship isn't healthy (Scott 2023). A healthy friendship is one in which both people respect each other's boundaries and are able to communicate openly without fearing the consequences (Degges-White 2018). Boundaries are crucial, they define personal space and self-preservation in any relationship. For example, in a healthy friendship you should be able to say "No" to plans when you need downtime or refuse to engage in gossip that makes you uncomfortable.

Friendships need to be developed and nurtured, and this is an ongoing process that requires effort and intention from both people. The best way to make sure this happens is to make sure that you regularly check in with each other. Maybe it's a quick coffee date or maybe it's a long video call. The situation doesn't matter as long as it helps you keep the bond between you alive. The time you spend together doesn't always have to be one-on-one, though. Group activities and clubs can also strengthen friendships by giving you a chance to create shared experiences and memories and explore your interests together. Better yet, you'll have an opportunity to meet new people at the same time as deepening your existing relationships.

It's at this point that we should talk about peer pressure because this often lurks in social situations like the ones we're talking about, and it can subtly influence your decisions, sometimes pulling you in directions you might not want to go. You can handle it; you're just going to need a bit of confidence and a strong sense of self. Your goal is to be able to say a firm "No" to anything that makes you uncomfortable. You'll need to communicate assertively and express your refusal without being aggressive or apologizing for yourself. For instance, if you're pressured to try something you're uncomfortable with, you can respond honestly but kindly by saying something like, "I'm not interested in doing that." You can make this easier on yourself by thinking of scenarios where peer pressure might arise—at parties, group outings, or casual hangouts, for example—and mentally rehearsing your responses.

Friendship Audit Checklist

Take a moment to reflect on your friendships by considering the following questions and applying them to each one:

1. Does this friendship make me feel valued and respected?
2. Are my boundaries acknowledged and respected?
3. Do we share common interests and values?

Once you have your answers, you have some insight into the health of each friendship, and if you feel like any of them are lacking, you can start working on improving them. This won't always be possible, though, and it's okay to distance yourself from friendships that no longer serve you positively. This is an act of self-care, and it will preserve your emotional well-being. You'll be better off looking for connections that resonate with who you are and who you aspire to be. You want to be surrounded by friends who encourage your growth, celebrate your achievements, and provide you with unwavering support.

Non-Verbal Communication Cues

What you hear when you walk into a busy room is chatter, but there's also another way the people in that room are communicating. They're using their body language. Body language is at work in every interaction you have, and when you know how to use it effectively, it can add power to the words you speak. Being able to read it is just as important, though. For instance, a slouched posture could be a sign of disinterest, or it might convey an underlying fatigue or discomfort, while a slight lean forward typically indicates attentiveness and an eagerness to connect on a deeper level. Subtle signs like maintained eye contact, frequent nods, or mirrored actions can speak volumes about someone's engagement, and you may be able to spot discomfort or disagreement through crossed arms or eyes that wander (Cherry 2025).

Let's say you're walking into an unfamiliar group setting. You want to seem confident and approachable, and scary as it may be, one of the best ways you can do this is to maintain eye contact. You'll immediately communicate that you're fully present and engaged in the moment, and this can facilitate trust and help you to build immediate connections. You can take this to the next level by pairing it with open gestures, uncrossed arms and a relaxed posture to send out a clear message of approachability and self-assurance. Try to let your gestures flow seamlessly as extensions of your speech, punctuating the most important points without over-shadowing the conversation. Even something as simple as nodding can keep conversation flowing and reassure the person speaking of your engagement and interest. See? Active listening is helpful in every context!

One important thing to point out is that nonverbal communication is not the same in every culture. A gesture that seems friendly in one place might be misunderstood elsewhere. Take the thumbs up, for example. In many Western countries, it signals approval, but in parts of the Middle East and West Africa, it can be seen as offensive (Anderson et. al. 2019). This is why understanding the cultural context of your audience matters. Misunderstandings caused by these differences can create awkward situations, so learning about them shows respect and builds stronger connections.

In settings like parties or group meetings, non-verbal cues can help you gauge the collective mood of the group. You've probably been in a room before where you've been able to feel the tension. You'll see it through furrowed eyebrows and crossed arms, and it's a striking contrast to a lively space where everyone's leaning forward and sharing eye contact. When you can spot this, you can modify your behavior appropriately. If the group exudes energy, resonating with that enthusiasm will help you to blend in and feel a part of it. If, on the other hand, the environment is more subdued, approaching the group with a serene demeanor may fit the tone better.

Reading body language can also help you draw other people into the group. Have you ever been in a study session where one person has dominated and everyone else has been silent? If you can detect cues like eye rolls or sighs from quieter members of the group, you'll know that they're not happy, and you can make an extra effort to encourage their contribution, which may be enough to rebalance the group.

Seriously, understanding body language is a powerful skill. Pay attention, and I'm sure you'll start to see how much reading it will help every interaction you have.

Resolving Conflicts Respectfully

I'm sure you're familiar with conflict. It's an inevitable part of any relationship. Conflict in itself isn't a problem; what matters is how you handle it. The worst thing you can do is ignore it because when you let tensions simmer beneath the surface, they eventually boil over and become bigger issues. Conflicts in friendships can arise from misunderstandings, differing opinions, or unmet expectations, and they can range from simple disagreements over where to hang out to more complex issues like betrayals of trust (Gordon 2019). To resolve conflicts in a healthy way, issues like this must be addressed directly and constructively, no matter how tempted you are to avoid them (Army Cadets n.d.). When you face them head-on, you can solve the immediate problem at the same time as strengthening the friendship by showing that it's resilient enough to weather disagreements.

To do this, however, you're going to need to be able to communicate effectively, and, in my opinion, the best trick here is to use "I" statements. Have you ever caught yourself saying something like, "You never listen?" This is going to get the other person's back up immediately. A better solution would be to say something like, "I feel unheard when I'm interrupted." Can you see how the focus has now shifted from blame to expressing your feelings and experiences? The other person is far less likely to be defensive now (Robbins n.d.). You'll also have to be careful to listen without interrupting. This shows respect for the other person's perspective and allows both of you the chance to understand the issue more clearly. When both parties feel heard, they're more likely to approach the conflict with empathy and open-mindedness, laying the groundwork for resolution (Chastain 2013).

It's difficult to find common ground when you're in the middle of a conflict, but it's essential if you want to reach an amicable resolution. Start by identifying shared goals or values that both of you can agree on. This could be as simple as wanting the friendship to continue or agreeing on mutual respect as a priority. Once you've pinpointed these values, you can start to brainstorm solutions together. Now you're collaborating, and this will allow you to generate more ideas and give you a sense of joint ownership over the resolution process. Compromise and negotiation are super important here—sometimes it's about meeting in the middle or giving a little to get a little. You may not get exactly what you want, but if you come to a compromise, you're doing well, and both of you will feel valued and respected.

Once the dust of the conflict has settled, your next focus is to repair the relationship. This is where apologizing for any harsh words or actions comes in—and I don't just mean saying, "I'm sorry." For your apology to mean something, you must acknowledge your role in the conflict and express a desire to make amends (Joshi n.d.). An apology note can be a thoughtful way to convey your sincerity and reflection, and some people find this approach easier. Sometimes, putting pen to paper allows you to articulate your thoughts more clearly than speaking in the heat of the moment. Rebuilding trust, however, takes time and consistent effort, and you'll need to demonstrate through your actions that you're committed to change and growth within the relationship.

You'll also need to be willing to communicate openly and check in regularly about how things are going once the conflict has died down. Be patient with the other person's healing process. Trust can't be restored overnight; it's earned through consistent, positive interactions, and you and your friend may need to set new boundaries or have regular check-ins to make sure you both feel secure and valued. Conflicts don't have to spell doom for friendships; on the contrary, they can be opportunities for deeper understanding and connection when you're able to handle them respectfully.

Expressing Yourself with Confidence

We often think of confidence as being loud, but it's really about allowing the authentic, bold, and beautiful shades of your personality to be seen and experienced by others. That doesn't mean you have to be loud about it. All you need to do is feel comfortable about sharing your thoughts, emotions, and ideas, without the looming fear of being ridiculed or judged harshly. This purposeful self-expression is really good for your personal development because it encourages you to explore and own your interests, values, and beliefs. It's also great for your social interactions because it allows you to make meaningful connections with people who admire and appreciate you for your true self.

This is where assertive communication comes in again, only this time, your goal is to convey your thoughts and feelings transparently and earnestly while respecting the viewpoints and emotions of others (Scott 2023). This isn't to be confused with aggressive communication, which typically disregards the feelings and perspectives of others (Scott 2023). You'll need to be able to control your tone and volume to do this; this way, your voice will be neither overpowering nor dismissive. Keep your tone calm and steady so that you're able to clearly communicate your message. You can practice this by speaking in front of a mirror or recording yourself. It might feel silly for a moment, but no one but you will know about it. What you're doing is increasing your self-awareness about how you sound, and this will help you to control your tone and delivery so that they match the circumstances and come across as assertive rather than aggressive.

I'm fully aware that you may have shyness and inhibitions to overcome, and this can be difficult, but trust me when I tell you that it will get easier with persistence and practice. Scary as it might seem, you can help yourself out by engaging in public speaking exercises. This is one of the things that James did to help his confidence, and it worked wonders. He joined a debate club, but it may be that a drama class would suit you better. Either way, it will boost your confidence in addressing an audience within a supportive environment where you can hone your ability to express your thoughts clearly and confidently. You can give yourself an extra boost by gradually broadening your social exposure if you tend to talk only to the people you feel safe with and trust. Try to break into more diverse social circles so that you get more comfortable with talking to different people. You can take your friends with you so that you feel safe and it's not so intimidating— just make sure you don't talk to them the whole time and avoid speaking with anyone new! As your confidence increases, you'll find it naturally easier to voice your thoughts and ideas in a wider variety of settings.

Nurturing Skills for Group Discussions

Expressing your opinions during group discussions can be intimidating, I know, but it's a good skill to build now. When you can articulate your thoughts skillfully, you'll feel more comfortable about participating, and it will pave the way for meaningful dialogue.

To effectively share your ideas in these settings, you'll need to be able to structure your arguments in a clear, logical format encompassing a beginning, a middle, and an end. You want to start with a compelling opening statement that captures the group's attention, then proceed with well-thought-out supporting points that back up what you're trying to say. But it isn't all about you. You'll also need to listen to other people's points of view respectfully and acknowledge their contributions. The idea is to create an environment in which every participant feels valued and appreciated so that the discussion is fruitful and enjoyable.

Mastering the art of confident self-expression brings benefits that extend far beyond social interactions. It will build your self-esteem and enhance your communication skills, and you'll probably find that it will strengthen your relationships. Expressing yourself confidently isn't about raising your voice or having all the right answers. It's about staying true to yourself and communicating this authenticity during every interaction.

Now, though, it's time for us to move on and explore a different area of powerful life skills. Yes, you can actually do this, even if organization isn't your thing. Get ready to take control of your schedule and make every moment count!

CHAPTER 4

EFFECTIVE TIME MANAGEMENT

"The key is in not spending time, but in investing it."

— STEPHEN R. COVEY

Have you ever found yourself racing to finish a project the night before it's due or studying frantically for an exam, only to run out of time before you can make it to the final chapter of the book? Yeah, me too. Not for a long time, though, and that's because I've worked on my time management skills. In this chapter, I'm going to share all the strategies I've used so that you, too, can become the master of your time.

The Eisenhower Matrix

You know those days that are so full you barely know whether you're coming or going? I'm talking about the kind of day when you have deadlines for school projects looming over you, soccer practice that you absolutely must go to, a family dinner, and a list of seemingly endless chores glaring at you. It's overwhelming, and you don't feel like you can give all of your energy to anything. The only thing to do is to prioritize.

Prioritizing means identifying what needs your immediate attention and what can wait, and you'd be amazed by how calming this can be. It means you can take a structured approach to your day, tackling your responsibilities methodically, which saves you a mountain of stress and makes you far more efficient at everything you need to do. The most effective way I've found to figure out where my priorities should be is to use the Eisenhower Matrix, sometimes known as a priority matrix.

The Eisenhower Matrix was developed by Dwight D. Eisenhower, the 34th president of the USA. It helps the user to visualize all their tasks according to how urgent and important they are, and it can include both smaller, daily tasks and larger projects. Each of these falls into one of four categories: urgent and important (tasks that need to be completed right away), not urgent and important (tasks that can come later on the calendar), urgent and unimportant (tasks that you could give to someone else), and not urgent and unimportant (tasks that you don't need to do at all). Once you have all of these tasks arranged in their categories, it becomes much easier to see what to prioritize (Scroggs n.d.).

Let's put this in context. If you have an assignment due the next day, you'd mark this as "urgent and important." Preparation for exams coming up in two weeks, however, might fall into the "not urgent and important" category. Washing the dishes, while it's a responsibility you shouldn't avoid, is something that someone other than you can do, so if you had to give all your time to your "urgent and important" task, you might be able to negotiate with someone else in your family for them to wash the dishes that night if you take their turn later in the week. Completing the final level of the video game you're playing, however, isn't a task you actually need to do (it's just something you *want* to do), and this can, therefore, be deleted. You can use it as a reward when you've finished your other tasks instead.

The Eisenhower Matrix looks like a grid segmented into four quadrants—one for each of the categories (Scroggs n.d.). You can get a feel for how it works right now. Grab a pencil and paper, and divide the sheet into four quadrants. Now start to methodically sort through your responsibilities for the week, placing each one into its appropriate category. You should be able to clearly see which tasks you should prioritize and make decisions according to which things are the most important. You can plan your daily and weekly schedules according to your priorities. Bear in mind that these will change week to week, though. You'll need to come back to your matrix and shuffle the tasks as new things get added and deadlines come closer. Regularly revisiting and reshuffling your priorities like this will help you to stay true to your objectives. Life never stands still, and neither should your approach to managing it.

Weekly Prioritization Review Schedule

Dedicate a portion of your week to thoroughly reviewing your prioritization matrix. Reflect on your achievements over the week while you plan for the tasks ahead, and think carefully about whether you need to prioritize differently.

You may find those old feelings of overwhelm creeping back in when new tasks pop up. The secret to dealing with this is to stay flexible and ask for help when you need it. Try to stay calm, revisit your matrix, and think carefully about how you can keep the balance while accommodating your new responsibilities.

You'll get better at this over time, and the more you practice, the better you'll set yourself up for the future. You'll always need to prioritize things, and this is a valuable skill to learn now.

Time-Blocking

Imagine beginning each day with a sense of calm and certainty. Wouldn't that be something? You wake up, and from the start, there's no scramble, no confusion—just a clear plan detailing the purpose of every chunk of time. You can make this happen, and to help you, you can use time-blocking.

Time-blocking is essentially about dividing your day into distinct segments, or "blocks," each one assigned to a specific task or activity. When you get good at this, you'll find that your productivity surges, your stress diminishes, and suddenly, those insurmountable tasks don't seem so daunting. In short, you'll be in control, and you'll be able to give each task the attention it deserves.

To do this well, you're going to need to think carefully about your natural rhythms. We all have those moments when our alertness peaks and our productivity surges—the golden hours when our cognitive capabilities are maximized. Pinpoint these periods within your day. There's not much you can do differently when these moments are times that you're in class, but you can still use them on the weekends and during the school breaks. Some people are at their most productive first thing in the morning, but for other people, the late afternoon is when they find they get the most done. Decide what your prime windows are, and work on your most demanding tasks during these times. If you're preparing for an upcoming exam, for example, or working on a detailed project, this is work you'll want to block into your most productive hours. You can then insert buffer times between these blocks—brief breaks to allow you to recharge and refresh. Don't leave these breaks out of your schedule. They'll help you to reset and preserve your energy throughout the day so that you stay focused and keep up the momentum (Perry 2022).

Time-blocking can completely change the way you approach each day, and I highly recommend you try it. Print off a weekly calendar where each day is divided into hours, and then start planning out each day, blocking off the time where you're at school or committed to another activity first. With the hours that are left, you might take an hour for concentrated academic work, followed by a 15-minute break to stretch and refresh. Perhaps the next hour will be spent on a hobby or a workout session before dinner. Life, as I'm sure you know, is intrinsically unpredictable, so you'll need to be adaptable. Should an unforeseen task or event come up, you'll need to rework your time blocks to accommodate it.

You need to make sure your schedule includes both fixed commitments and flexible activities. This means considering your class times, sports practices, and any other responsibilities so you can clearly see how much time is available. Once these key items are in place, you can easily add study sessions, social plans, and time to relax. The goal is not to fill every minute, but to use your time wisely, giving important tasks the attention they need while still leaving room for fun. As you get used to this approach, you will start to find a rhythm that fits your lifestyle. This rhythm will help you stay focused on your goals while remaining open to unexpected opportunities.

Digital Time-Blocking Tools

If all of this pencil and paper is a bit too much like hard work for you, you can use digital tools to help you block your time. I recommend Google Calendar and Trello. Both tools give you the option to color-code your tasks so that you can see them clearly, and you can set reminders and share your schedule when you need to collaborate with other people on a project. If you're thinking about using a different platform, choose one that shows your full day clearly so you can easily see what needs to change and stay in control. You might also want to consider apps with cross-device syncing abilities to make sure you can access your schedule wherever you are.

I've heard good things about "Todoist" and "Notion," which are both known for their user-friendly designs and robust customization settings. Both platforms include task prioritization features and seamless integration with other productivity applications, so these could be good ones to investigate, too.

Avoiding Procrastination

Have you ever found yourself staring at a blank page, knowing you should start your homework, but every fiber of your being screams for another episode of your favorite show? That's the sneaky grip of procrastination, a habit that keeps many people from their tasks in a way that, ultimately, adds stress to their lives. The first step to tackling this is to work out what triggers it.

For many people, emotional triggers like fear of failure or self-doubt are to blame. You might avoid starting something because you're worried it won't be perfect, and you might not even be conscious of the fact that this is the reason (Cherry 2024). You may also be distracted by environmental factors like a cluttered workspace or noisy surroundings, which may lead you to start doing something other than the task you're meant to be focused on. If you can identify what your triggers are, you'll be able to work on your environment and mindset so that they encourage you to be more productive.

If you're struggling to stay focused on a task right now, take a moment to think about what's causing your procrastination. Then you can develop a solid action plan, and that should begin by breaking it down into bite-sized, manageable steps. This will make a big project less intimidating and more achievable. List all the steps you're going to need to work through in order to complete a task, then set specific deadlines for each one. Let's say you're working on a research paper, for example. You could break it into stages like topic selection, outline creation, research gathering, and writing drafts. You can then set a realistic deadline for each step, which will allow you to make steady progress without feeling overwhelmed. This structured approach will keep you on track and build your confidence as you tick off each completed step.

I know what you're thinking—surely now you just have a lot more things you can procrastinate about! But procrastination will be less likely when you're not looking at one massive project and each part seems more manageable (Yeung 2021). You can also employ a few other techniques to help you avoid procrastination. The Pomodoro Technique is one of my favorites. The idea is that you work in short, focused bursts—typically 25 minutes—followed by a brief break. This way, you'll be able to maintain your concentration and avoid burnout because your brain is getting regular rest intervals (Scroggs n.d.).

Consider forming an accountability partnership, which is simpler than it sounds. All you need to do is partner up with a friend or classmate who has a similar goal, and check in with them regularly to discuss your progress and the challenges each of you is facing. Knowing that someone else is counting on you can boost your motivation and keep procrastination at bay (Hope-Jones 2023).

It will also help you to develop a proactive mindset, which means anticipating obstacles before they become roadblocks and preparing for them accordingly. Visualization exercises can be a powerful tool for staying motivated. Imagine yourself finishing tasks and reaching your goals, feeling that sense of satisfaction when you finally complete a project or succeed on an exam. These mental images can give you the push you need when procrastination tries to take control (Price 2017).

Building a proactive mindset also involves cultivating habits that support sustained productivity. Establish a routine that works with your natural rhythms and preferences. If you're a morning person, tackle your most challenging tasks first thing in the morning when your energy is high, just as we discussed when we were talking about time blocking. If you're a night owl, try to schedule the most demanding activities later in the day when your focus is at its best. Of course, you'll still need to be adaptable and willing to adjust your plans when unexpected changes or new priorities arise.

Your environment matters too. You want it to be conducive to productivity, and it's surprising how much this can help with procrastination. Organize your workspace so that there are minimal distractions and you can focus better. This will mean keeping all the equipment you need within reach while removing unnecessary clutter that might distract you. If you have the space, you can even divide your room into specific areas for different activities—study zones, relaxation corners, and creative spaces, for example—to cue yourself mentally into the right mindset for each task.

You're going to need to show yourself compassion during this process. Everyone experiences moments of delay, and it's okay to stumble occasionally. Instead of criticizing yourself for procrastination that's already happened, focus on the present moment and the steps you can take to be productive now. Celebrate each small victory so that you notice what you're doing well just as much as you notice the things you'd like to improve. Finished reading a chapter of your study guide? Then celebrate it. Completed the first draft of a paper? Celebrate it. You'll soon start to see that you're achieving more than you think you are.

Some incredible people have been chronic procrastinators, and they still managed to achieve great things. Mozart, da Vinci, and Steve Jobs are just a handful of them, and no one would argue that they haven't left their mark on their world (Shatz n.d.). Taking control of our time and actions leads to extraordinary results, and anyone can conquer procrastination if they set their mind to it.

Balancing School, Hobbies, and a Social Life

You have a ton of responsibilities, interests, and people vying for your attention. School demands your attention, your hobbies need you to practice, and there are invites and gatherings galore. So, how do you balance so many things?

The first thing to do is assess your current commitments. Create a commitment inventory that lists every activity and responsibility that occupies your time. You should include school assignments, club meetings, sports practices, and social engagements—it's all taking your time, even the fun stuff. Once you have it all laid out, you can look for places where your time might be slipping away from you. Are there activities that take up more time than they should? If you want to gain control over your schedule, you're going to need to be able to spot the time-wasters.

Now that you have a clear picture of where your time is going, you can start implementing strategies to balance your commitments effectively. One approach is to synchronize your calendar to integrate school responsibilities with leisure activities. Use a digital calendar or planner to schedule study sessions alongside your hobbies so that you can be sure that both are getting their fair share of your attention. Your time blocking will help you with this, too, of course. You can set specific time slots for social interactions so that you can enjoy moments with your friends without letting your academic performance slip. You'll need to be clear about your boundaries: Designate particular days or times for socializing, and stick to them. It may not be what you really want to do a lot of the time, but it will help you to keep that balance and make sure that you're still doing well in school.

Setting personal boundaries isn't just about managing your time, it's about safeguarding your well-being, too. You need personal time to avoid burnout and create a balanced life—and this isn't time with friends, but moments that are truly just for you. Make sure you have time each week for the activities that recharge you like reading, working-out, meditating, walking, or whatever is your jam. This might mean that you'll need to get good at saying, "No," and the work we did on peer pressure will help. It's okay to turn down an invitation if it conflicts with your need for rest or other priorities, and you need to be able to do this in order to protect your mental and emotional health (Nash 2018).

Again, life is unpredictable, and the demands on your time will change every now and then. This means that it would be a good idea to set aside time each week to evaluate how well you're balancing school, hobbies, and your social life. Ask yourself questions like, "Am I dedicating enough time to my studies?" or "Have I been able to enjoy my hobbies without feeling rushed?" If you ask yourself questions like this regularly, you'll be able to identify any areas that need adjustment and fine-tune your routine accordingly.

As your priorities change whether because of a new school project or a growing passion for a hobby you will need to stay flexible and adjust your schedule accordingly. You need to be flexible. If an unanticipated opportunity arises, like attending a special event or joining a new club, for example, assess its impact on your existing commitments. You might need to make minor adjustments to make sure that your new opportunities aren't disrupting your balance.

Remember that achieving balance isn't about doing it all; it's about making choices that align with your values and goals and allow you to keep your mental health steady. This should all be much easier with the tools you've picked up in this chapter. Next, we're going to move on to financial literacy, which I know isn't everyone's favorite topic—but trust me, you want to know about it, and I think you'll find it's more interesting than you fear.

CHAPTER 5

FINANCIAL LITERACY FOR TEENS

"Do not save what is left after spending, but spend what is left after saving."

— WARREN BUFFETT

If math isn't your strong suit, you might not be thrilled about this chapter. But hang in there—financial literacy isn't really about math. It's about understanding a concept that the world is built around... money. Sure, math comes into it here and there, but financial literacy isn't about calculations. It's about knowing how to make your money work for you, and if you want to be comfortable later in life, it's a skill you need now.

Creating Your First Budget

What happens when you get your monthly allowance or your paycheck from a part-time job? Are you the sort of person who can't resist the temptation to splurge on the latest sneakers or a new gaming console? Don't feel bad. This happens to so many young people. But pause for a moment and consider this—what if you planned your spending better so that you'd still have some cash left when the next payday rolls around? It probably sounds impossible if you're used to your money disappearing as soon as you get it, but budgeting is here to save you. I won't claim that budgeting is the most exciting thing in the world, but it isn't as dull as you might fear, either, and it isn't complicated. It's really just about tracking your income and expenses, so you know exactly where your money is going and why you're saving it.

The first step is to understand where your money comes from and where it's going, so start by listing all your sources of income. You might get some from your allowance, some from a part-time job, or some from a side gig you've set up. Once you've sorted that, it's time to categorize your expenses. Think about what you spend on food, transportation, entertainment, and those tempting online shopping sprees. Jot them down in categories to see where most of your money flows. You might need to pay attention over the course of a month to figure this out if you've never given it much thought before. Once you're clear, you can start setting some financial goals. Are you saving for a new phone? Are there concert tickets you plan to buy? You want to make sure you have enough money to do these things, so by setting them as goals, you'll make it easier to control your spending in order to achieve them.

If this all sounds a bit daunting, don't worry. Technology is here to save the day! There are tons of apps out there designed to help with budgeting and saving. Apps like PocketGuard or YNAB are user-friendly and help you to track your spending and set financial goals (McMullen 2025). If you'd prefer something more hands-on, spreadsheets are a classic way to manage your budget. They give you the freedom to customize your categories and calculations however you like. Digital tools are convenient, but sometimes you can't beat the basic power of a pen and paper—sometimes jotting things down manually can make the whole thing feel more real.

The truth is, budgeting is not something you do just once. To stay on track, you need to review it regularly. Make time each month to look over your budget and see how things are going. Did you stick to your spending limits? Were there unexpected expenses that threw off your plan? By regularly reviewing and adjusting your budget, you'll learn how to adapt to changes in your income or expenses without losing control. If an unplanned expense pops up, like an emergency car repair, for example, evaluate where you can cut back temporarily to accommodate it. This doesn't mean you have to limit yourself, it's about making intentional choices that support what truly matters to you and chances are right now, there are a few things draining your cash that you don't really care about.

Monthly Budget Review Checklist

Take a moment each month to evaluate your finances using this checklist:

- Did I meet my savings goals?
- Where did I overspend?
- Are there subscriptions I can cancel or reduce?
- What will I need to adjust for next month?

This might all seem a bit tedious at first, but it will become second nature once you get the hang of it. You'll start feeling more in control and confident about your financial decisions, and the review process will gradually become quicker and easier.

Credit

Credit is essentially a contractual agreement that allows you to borrow money with a clear understanding that this amount will be returned later, generally accompanied by an added cost known as interest. There are several different kinds of credit, each one tailored to serve a distinct need, such as credit cards, student loans, auto loans, or personal loans. Each type comes with a unique set of regulations and guidelines, closely linked to the specific financial journey it supports. Think of credit like trust— just as people earn trust by keeping their promises, you build good credit by paying back what you borrow on time. This trust with lenders can open doors to more opportunities and better financial options in the future.

Once you start using credit, you'll need to pay attention to something called your credit score. This is a three-digit number rating your creditworthiness and affecting your ability to qualify for loans or credit cards. It's based on your credit history, which includes the accounts you have, how much debt you're carrying, and your repayment history (Investopedia 2025). If you have a strong credit score, you're more likely to be eligible for favorable loan conditions and reduced interest rates, and this is important because it makes the process of big things like purchasing a car or a home much more straightforward.

I know all of this probably seems intimidating, but if you're diligent and responsible, you'll plant a firm foundation for your financial well-being. If you're new to credit, the best way to get started is with secured credit cards. What's special about these is that they require an upfront deposit, which essentially serves as your credit limit and gives the lender security in case you can't make your payments (Segal 2025). They're good for building your credit history without running the risk of overspending. It's a bit like when you first learn to swim and you always get in the pool with a float: It gives you a chance to learn while you still have a safety net.

Another option is to use a co-signer, someone financially responsible who agrees to take over your debt if you cannot make the payments (Waugh 2024). This might be your parents, grandparents, or some other financially secure family member. This is a way you can begin to establish credit without taking any significant risk, as long as you manage your expenses carefully and make sure you pay your bills on time.

Savings

Credit allows you to borrow money in order to pay for the things you need and then pay that debt back over time. With saving, it works the other way around—you're making payments into your savings account *before* you need to use the money. This does take foresight and planning, though.

Saving can be divided into two fundamental categories: short-term and long-term savings. Short-term savings cover immediate or upcoming expenses, things like buying a new bicycle or funding an overseas adventure with your friends. Long-term savings are aimed at achieving more substantial goals, typically involving saving up for five years or more, such as paying for college tuition or purchasing a new vehicle. The difference basically comes down to the time frame (FNB n.d.). The great thing about saving money over time is that you get back more than what you put into it. This is the magic of compound interest. You earn interest on the original amount you put into the account, and you also earn interest on your interest (Fernando 2024).

When you don't have a lot of money, saving sometimes seems impossible, but you'd be surprised. There are a few strategies you can use to help you. One of my favorites is the 50/30/20 rule. The idea is that you allocate 50% of your income for necessities, 30% for discretionary spending (the things you want), and the remaining 20% for savings and repaying any debt (Ayoola n.d.). If you can implement this strategy, saving will become a habitual practice, and you'll be able to work toward your financial goals without feeling like you're depriving yourself. Another option is to use savings plans, which basically put your savings on autopilot. You set it up so that a fixed amount of money is automatically transferred from your checking account to your savings account every month. This way, you can make sure you're saving without having to put much thought into it, and you avoid the temptation of immediate spending.

Smart Spending Decisions

The struggle between wants and needs is real. You might think that you really need a new pair of sneakers, but do you? Or do you just *want* them? It might sound obvious, but being able to recognize the difference between needs and wants can transform how you handle your money. Needs are essential for survival and daily functioning—groceries, rent, and school supplies. Wants, on the other hand, are those nice-to-haves like that new video game or dinner at a fancy restaurant. The sneakers could fall into either category. If your old ones have holes in the soles, you probably need some new ones. If they're in perfectly good condition and there's just a new style out that you like, you probably just want them. Your job is to identify which category they fall into so you can start making informed decisions and making sure you're using your hard-earned cash wisely.

Once you have this figured out, you can set up a spending plan, which is basically like setting rules for yourself. Start by setting spending limits for different categories. Allocate a certain amount of money for essentials and another for fun stuff. To do this well, you're going to need to track your spending. Monitor where each dollar goes so you're always sure you're staying within your set limits. If you tend to lose track, it might be a good idea to use a money management app. Many of these offer features like spending alerts, which will give you a gentle reminder when you're about to overshoot your budget.

When you're considering buying something, think carefully. Consider the item's cost, whether you really need it, and how much value it has in the long term. The "24-hour rule" is a handy trick—if you find something you think you must have, wait a day before you commit to buying it. This will give you time to consider if it's really worth it or if it's just an impulse. Calculating the cost-per-use is another smart move. If you're buying a pricey jacket, for example, consider how often you'll wear it. If you plan to use it every day, the investment might be worth it, but if it's something you'll wear once and then forget about, then maybe you should rethink that purchase.

Impulse buying tends to strike when your emotions are high— feeling bored, stressed, or even super happy can trigger it (Sundström et. al. 2013). The trick to resisting these triggers is to recognize them in the first place. Techniques like delayed gratification can help. This is essentially the process of resisting the temptation of an instant reward so that you can hold out for something better in the future (Maxabella 2022). Next time a flashy display at the mall tempts you, remind yourself of your financial goals. Try creating a wish list for things you want to buy in the future. It can help you stay focused and avoid impulse spending. When the urge to spend hits, you will have a clear reminder of what really matters to you. Also, take time to picture what financial success looks like in your life. It can keep you motivated and moving forward. It could be saving up for college or having enough to travel during the summer break. Keep this vision in your mind to motivate you when you're making spending decisions, and I'm sure you'll drastically reduce your unnecessary expenses.

It's okay to treat yourself occasionally, but do it mindfully. Allocate a small portion of your budget for guilt-free spending on wants, just as we discussed earlier. This way, you can enjoy fun stuff without it derailing your overall financial plan. The practice of mindful consumption will help you here, too. It just means being fully aware of why you're buying something and its impact on your finances and life satisfaction. It'll encourage you to make thoughtful decisions rather than spending on impulse.

You need to understand your spending habits, as if you're going to be able to make wise financial choices. When you understand what drives your decisions, it will be easier for you to control them. Try keeping a journal of your spending habits for a month. Write down what you spent your money on and why you bought it. You'll start to notice patterns and triggers that lead to unnecessary spending, and you'll probably see places where you could easily cut back.

Financial Independence Basics

Imagine a world in which you can make decisions without worrying about money. That's what financial independence is in a nutshell. It's a state in which your expenses are covered and you can chase your dreams without worrying about money. The best part is that economic freedom isn't just a dream or only for adults, but a goal you can start working towards now.

Financially independent people often display similar characteristics. They're disciplined, they're forward-thinking, and they have a knack for planning. They aren't stressed about bills because they've already built a solid foundation that supports their life-style. The amazing thing is that this kind of stability goes way beyond money. It's the key to living the life you want. It means you can focus on what really matters to you—whether that's traveling, studying, or starting your own business—and you can do it without constantly worrying about money.

To get there, you're going to need to set financial goals, and these will include both short-term and long-term goals, as we discussed earlier in the chapter. Short-term goals might be things like saving for a concert ticket or a new gadget. Long-term goals might be saving for college tuition or starting an emergency fund. Many teens, including my younger self, have found that making a finan-cial vision board is a fun and powerful way to focus on your goals and turbo charge your dreams into action. I carefully selected the exact images that represented my future goals and placed them on my vision board. By looking at it every day and truly visualizing myself already living that life, those dreams started becoming reality faster than I ever imagined. All you need to do is gather those images representing your financial dreams and arrange them on your vision board. It can be a physical board, on your screen, or both. Then every day, look at your vision board and imagine your-self already living that life. Your subconscious mind will keep reminding you of that purpose, driving you to act and stay moti-vated to follow your plan. It's an incredibly powerful tool!

Now, let's discuss how to start earning money to support these goals. There are plenty of opportunities out there if you know where to look. Part-time jobs at local stores or cafés are the obvious place to start, and they come with the added bonus of teaching you valuable skills like time management and customer service. Jobs like this will certainly pay. Internships, on the other hand, are often more of a long-term investment. They don't always pay, but even if they don't, they may help you, ultimately, to reach your goals by giving you insights into potential career paths while adding impressive experience to your resume. If you're more inclined towards flexibility, freelancing or online gigs could be your thing. Platforms like Fiverr or Upwork allow you to offer your services right from home, and these could be anything from graphic design to writing. And don't forget about entrepreneurship! You'd be surprised by the number of teenagers who've started businesses from their bedrooms, selling handmade crafts or tutoring services. Creativity and determination open up endless possibilities.

As you work on all of the principles we've been discussing in this chapter, you're going to be developing a financial mindset. You'll start valuing saving over spending, and you'll soon see money grow when because it's wisely managed. Financial education is key here, and I'd love you to keep pursuing it long after you close this book. There are countless resources: books, online courses, and workshops offering insights into financial literacy. Websites like Investopedia or Khan Academy provide free materials to boost your knowledge on everything from investing basics to economic principles, and they're great for checking things out when you're not too sure what a concept means.

As you can see, financial literacy isn't just about crunching numbers. In fact, there's very little number crunching involved. It's more about developing a mindset that values thoughtful decision-making and responsible resource management.

Financial independence is more than just having money; it's about the freedom it brings to live on your terms. And if you set clear goals, explore different income opportunities, and embrace a learning mindset, this is something you can achieve. Making wise decisions, as you know now, is an important part of this process, so in the next chapter, we'll delve into this skill specifically.

CHAPTER 6

DECISION-MAKING AND PROBLEM SOLVING

"It is our choices that show what we truly are, far more than our abilities."

— J.K. ROWLING

D id you know that we make, on average, about 35,000 decisions a day (Krockow 2018)? Most of them are so small you barely notice them. You choose oatmeal over toast, you choose to pour your coffee before you get the milk out of the fridge, you choose to sit at the kitchen table rather than on the couch... None of these decisions is all that important. Others, however, require more thought, and this is why decision-making is a skill you need to perfect. As you'll see later in the chapter, this also segues into problem solving. These are critical thinking skills, and they make all the difference to how well you're able to analyze information and make the best choices (Martins 2024).

The Decision-Making Process

Life throws countless decisions your way, from picking a college to choosing what to wear in the morning. Understanding the steps you take to make a decision can help you develop your skills so that you make thoughtful and well-informed choices.

Each decision you make is essentially a problem you have to solve. Let's take the seemingly innocuous decision we started with: choosing oatmeal over toast. The problem is that you don't know what to have for breakfast. By recognizing this, you've already completed the first step in making the decision: You've identified the problem. The next step is to gather information about the situation. What are your options? Oatmeal, toast, or eggs. You've already calculated that you don't have time to make eggs, so that one's wiped off the table before you've even considered it an option. That brings it down to oatmeal and toast. What's going to guide your decision? Is it as simple as going for the one you're most interested in right now? Probably not. Perhaps you have an exam today, and you know you're going to need sustained energy. Maybe you also know you're going to have a sandwich for lunch, and it would be a good idea to have something different rather than repeating bread. Problem solved! Oatmeal is the winner.

This process is relevant to every decision you make. You need to collect all the relevant facts, opinions, and data to make sure you make the right choice. Sometimes this might involve talking to friends or doing some research online. The more you know, the clearer your options will become.

Next comes evaluating your options, just like we did with the toast and the oatmeal. Weigh up the pros and cons of each one. Let's say you're deciding between joining a club and focusing on your studies. You'll need to consider how each option would fit with your priorities and long-term goals. With a decision like this, it might help you to use a visual aid like a decision-making flowchart so that you can clearly see each potential path. Making a chart like this will allow you to represent both options and their possible outcomes, and this will make it easier for you to see the connections and consequences.

This is where critical thinking plays an important role. You're aiming to analyze the information objectively, question your assumptions, and evaluate the evidence before you make a move (Martins 2024). Enhancing these skills involves asking open-ended questions and challenging your biases, all the while avoiding pitfalls like jumping to conclusions or relying solely on your gut feeling (Marr 2022). You always want logic and reason to guide your decisions.

Critical Thinking Techniques

The good news is that you can develop your critical thinking skills. There's an exercise called "Six Thinking Hats," where metaphorical hats represent different ways of thinking. The idea is that you try on each hat to look at the problem from multiple perspectives before you make your decision, looking at it from emotional, logical, and creative perspectives so that you have a well-rounded view (Hancock n.d.). Next time you have a big decision to make, I highly recommend looking this technique up.

When making a big decision, always keep your values and ethics in mind. Think about what matters most to you—honesty, kindness, integrity—and let those values guide your actions. Ethical dilemmas happen when your values clash with a situation. For instance, if your friend cheats on a test, you might feel torn between loyalty to your friend and your commitment to honesty. What would you choose? That decision is yours, but remember this: aligning your actions with your values builds integrity and makes it much easier to live comfortably with your choices.

Assessing your personal values will help you to clearly see where you stand. Reflect on decisions you've made in the past that made you feel proud or uneasy, and identify the values that were at play when you made them. You can use this information to help guide your future choices. When you're faced with an ethical dilemma like the one in our example, ask yourself if your decision resonates with your core beliefs.

It's a good idea to set clear objectives before you make any decision. This will make sure you stay in line with your goals. Define what you want to achieve from a choice—is it academic success, personal growth, or social connection? Once you know what this is, you can write a decision objective statement so that you have a clear idea of what you want to achieve. This way, you'll think about how each choice affects your life and goals, and you'll have a clear vision of what you want to achieve. For instance, if you're choosing between extracurricular activities, an objective might be, "I want to join activities that will improve my leadership skills."

As you can see decision making isn't just choosing between A and B it's an art that combines logic values and goals, even when deciding what to have for breakfast!

Evaluating Options and Consequences

The expression "standing at a crossroad" is used more often as a metaphor to describe trying to make significant life decisions than it is about physical crossroads. This happens because no matter how hard we try to control our lives, unexpected twists and turns appear that force us to make choices. Often, one option is to stay as we are, taking the comfortable and familiar road. One path takes you into the unknown offering new adventures and opportunities which might feel exciting but scary. When faced with a choice like this, how do you decide which path to follow?

Brainstorming

My favorite strategy in this situation is brainstorming. It gives me a chance to freely explore all possibilities while feeling in control and removing limitations I unknowingly place on myself. If you want to try this, start by seeing every thought as valuable. Even the ideas that seem wild or impractical might contain the seed of something truly worthwhile. To visualize this clearly, write your dilemma in the center of a piece of paper and surround it with bubbles representing each idea you explore. This method works for anything from choosing a college major to planning your next vacation, and you might be surprised by the creative solutions you uncover.

Exploring the Pros and Cons

Brainstorming is a great way to get a good idea of all the possibilities, but you still have to evaluate each one. This is where the pros and cons list comes into play. What you're essentially doing is giving each option a mental test drive so that you can imagine your potential future with each of them. Let's say you were trying to decide whether to take a gap year before college—weighing up the pros and cons of doing so would help you to see how it might pan out if you did. Would it be a year of personal growth and discovery, or might it involve challenges and setbacks? You'd also want to weigh up what would happen if you went straight to college. You'd get your qualification more quickly, and you'd still be in a studying mindset, but you might not get a chance to travel or try new things. Thinking through each pro and con carefully will help you to understand the short-term and long-term consequences of each option. What you're trying to do is paint a broad yet detailed picture that includes what you stand to gain and what sacrifices might be required along the way.

Balancing Risks and Rewards

Each option is likely to come with risks and rewards, and your next job is to compare them and see how they balance. There's nothing wrong with taking risks. In fact, it's good for you—it builds your confidence, increases your resilience, and helps you to grow (Cooks-Campbell 2022). But there's no sense in choosing an option that comes with a huge amount of risk and not much reward. Let's consider a new example: deciding whether to choose a trade school instead of going to college. If you had no clear idea about which trade to pursue or didn't research the available career opportunities, you might risk losing valuable time or money. However, if you take time to explore your skills, interests, and the different trades available, you might discover rewarding career paths that align perfectly with your strengths. Choosing a trade school could open doors to excellent job prospects and financial independence earlier in life. Taking this informative approach can help you make a smart, balanced decision about your future.

Structuring Your Decisions

If you're thinking that all of this brainstorming and weighing up of options sounds a bit chaotic, you're right. That's why you need some structure in your decision-making process, and for this part, I'm going to ask you to think a bit like a business owner. The tool I want to introduce you to now is a decision-making model often used in business: a decision matrix. A decision matrix is a grid that allows you to compare the features of each option side by side. It's up to you what factors you consider, but you might consider cost, time commitment, and alignment with your personal goals. You would draw a grid with each of these options heading a column, and then rate your options side by side in the spaces below (Martins 2025). Let's say you are choosing between two summer internships and use a decision matrix to compare them. You might find that one offers a higher paycheck, while the other provides valuable experience related to your career goals. A clear structure like this makes it easier to weigh the pros, cons, risks, and benefits before making a decision.

The thing about big decisions is that they're never easy, but it all becomes a whole lot easier when you have some structure for the decision-making process. Approach it logically like this, and you should end up feeling confident in your decision.

Problem-Solving Strategies

There's a strong link between decision-making and problem-solving, and problems are an inevitable part of life. Every day presents a series of puzzles that require solving, ranging from so small that you barely notice them to so large that it's easy to feel panicked. It's easy to get caught up in addressing the symptoms rather than digging into the root cause when a problem feels this big. Have you ever heard of the "5 Whys" technique? This will help you here.

It's very simple: You just ask yourself, "Why?" five times, stripping away superficial issues until you hit the core problem (Toneva n.d.). For instance, if you're consistently late to school, you might start by asking why you leave home late. The answer might be that you struggle to wake up on time. So why do you struggle to wake up on time? Perhaps because you go to bed too late. Why do you go to bed too late? Maybe it's because you always seem to take a long time to do your homework. Why is homework taking so long?

Perhaps it's because you find it hard to concentrate, and you spend a lot of time procrastinating. Why is that happening? Is it because your desk is cluttered and there are distractions everywhere? There you have it: By asking yourself, "Why?" five times and exploring the issue deeply, you've uncovered the fact that the surprising reason you keep being late to school is because your room is a mess! Now you have a solution: Tidy your room! I truly adore this technique because it encourages you to look beyond the obvious to uncover the underlying causes of a problem. Then, the solutions are sometimes very surprising and help to give you clarity to get out of a bind.

Once you've identified the core issue, it's time to come up with creative solutions. This is where your creativity gets to shine. In our example, the solution was quite straightforward, but sometimes, traditional methods just won't cut it, and you'll need to be more creative. Lateral thinking exercises are a good way to get your creative juices flowing. They can help spark new ideas by encouraging you to think of unconventional approaches. Look some up online—they're quite fun! Mind mapping might help you, too. It's just like brainstorming: Write your central problem in the center of your map, and let your ideas branch out like the limbs of a tree. Just as with brainstorming, every thought is valuable, so let them roam freely without judging them, and try to capture every possibility before you start narrowing them down.

Next, it is time to evaluate the possible solutions and put the best ones into action. Not every idea will be a perfect fit, and that is completely fine. What matters is setting clear criteria to guide your decision. You might evaluate your options based on factors such as feasibility, cost, time, and overall impact. If you were shopping for a new phone, you wouldn't just grab the first one you saw. You'd compare features, prices, and reviews before making a purchase. That's what you're going to do with your potential solutions, too.

Weigh your options against your criteria to identify the most promising solution. Once you've chosen one, you can come up with an action plan detailing the steps you'll need to take in order to implement it.

Remember, no solution is permanent. Keep an eye on the results and make sure your choice is working the way you planned. In business, they use key performance indicators (KPIs) to measure success, and you could use these too. Yours might be things like improved grades or reduced stress levels. Regularly check these indicators to see if your solution is working. If your goal was for your solution to make you feel less stressed out, and you're noticing no change, you probably didn't choose the best solution, and it's time to go back to the drawing board. Things don't always go to plan, but don't panic—consider it an opportunity for growth. Keep tweaking and refining your approach until you solve the problem in a way that satisfies you.

Mind Mapping Exercise

Do you currently have a problem plaguing you? Then why not try out mind mapping right now? Grab a blank sheet and start mind mapping the problem. Write it in the center of the page, and let your ideas branch out organically. You might be surprised by the solutions that emerge when you let creativity lead.

Learning from Your Mistakes

Mistakes are part of life. They're often annoying, and it's easy to beat ourselves up for making them, but they're actually really good for our personal development (Harvey n.d.). When you make a mistake, you might feel frustrated or embarrassed at first, but these feelings won't last forever, and, ironically, it's precisely this mistake that may lead to a memorable and transformative lesson.

To feel more comfortable with making mistakes, the best thing you can do is reframe them as opportunities for learning and growth. Consider the often-quoted words of Thomas Edison. He famously said, "I have not failed. I've just found 10,000 ways that won't work" (Thomas Edison Foundations n.d.). Even the most accomplished people have experienced their share of setbacks en route to fulfilling their aspirations. Reflect, for a moment, on mistakes from your past. Perhaps you bombed a test you felt prepared for or overlooked a critical deadline with significant consequences. I bet you'll find that you learned something in the process that helped you prepare for similar situations in the future. Mistakes can be some of your greatest learning opportunities!

Analyzing Your Mistakes Constructively

If you want to make the most of the lessons a mistake can offer, you're going to need to get into the habit of analyzing them. There's a concept borrowed from medical examinations called a "post-mortem" analysis, in which you thoroughly review what went wrong and the reasons it happened (Jaworski 2024). The goal is not to get stuck on your failures, it is to learn from them and gain a deeper understanding that helps you grow for future developments.

To conduct a post-mortem analysis, all you need to do is ask yourself some questions: What was your initial goal? What actions or steps did you take, and at what point did they start to take you off down the wrong path? You can get a lot of insight from doing this action, and you might want to make a "lessons learned" document so that you can keep track of everything. Another reason why journaling can be very helpful!

Building Resilience through Adversity

Making mistakes builds your resilience (Harvey n.d.). When you face setbacks directly and look for the lessons within them, you strengthen your ability to bounce back. This will happen naturally, but to really amply the effect, you might try journaling or talking things through with a friend to help you process your emotions about the challenge and come up with coping strategies. There are many stories of people who turned adversity into success, so let their journeys inspire you. For example, J.K. Rowling faced countless rejections from publishers long before Harry Potter became a worldwide phenomenon (Hall n.d.). Imagine what would have happened if she had given up, but she did not. She used those rejections to build her resilience, and now the whole world knows her name.

Applying the Lessons You Learn

You can truly see the power of mistakes when you're able to apply the insights you've taken from them to inform better decision-making in the future. To really see your progress in a tangible way, you might want to come up with a personal improvement plan, plotting specific actions that are informed by your prior experiences. Establish clear, strategic goals, and diligently track your progress. You might decide to stick to a routine studying schedule to avoid the pressures of pre-exam cramming, or you might set reminders to avoid missing deadlines. Your written plan will make it easier to track your progress. Remember to acknowledge and celebrate those small wins along the way, as they will remind you how far you have come.

Mistakes are intrinsic to the human experience. They shape your identity and lay the foundation for the person you are yet to become—so stop feeling bad about them, and start using them to your advantage!

In the next chapter, we're going to change course and think about the digital world. There are many mistakes that can be made there, and as much as you can learn from them, in some cases, it's better just to avoid them altogether!

CHAPTER 7

DIGITAL LITERACY AND ONLINE SAFETY

"It's not about how many followers you have, but about how many lives you touch."

— SHAWN MENDES

A couple of decades ago, this chapter would not have existed. Digital literacy and online safety were not essential life skills because the digital world was nothing like it is today. Now, these skills are crucial, and you will need them both now and in the future.

Your Digital Footprint

It's probably a daily occurrence for you to casually browse the internet, scrolling through your social media feeds, liking a few posts here and there, and leaving a comment on a discussion or sharing an article that resonated with you. It all seems very innocuous, but beneath the surface, something much larger is happening—each click, share, like, and comment is contributing to what is known as your digital footprint. But what exactly is a digital footprint?

Essentially, it's the trail that you leave behind as you peruse the internet, and it isn't always visible. This digital trail is constructed through every one of your online activities, whether you've done them consciously (such as when you deliberately post a photo on social media) or unconsciously (like when your search history in a search engine is automatically logged). Every digital action contributes to this footprint, sculpting how you're seen in the digital universe (BBC Bitesize n.d.).

Every post you share on social media slowly becomes a part of your digital identity, and even if you delete something, traces can still remain online. Your search history is also a powerful record of your interests, questions, and habits. If someone were to look through everything you have searched, from those late-night questions driven by curiosity to your repeated attempts to solve a challenging math problem, they could discover far more about you than you might expect. What you search for online can reveal personal details about your interests, your curiosity, and the way you think, making it important to understand how much of your digital life is visible to others.

The long-term impact of your digital footprint isn't something to be taken lightly. It extends far beyond casual online interactions and fleeting digital connections. Notably, in academia and employment, where college admissions officers and potential employers tend to be very diligent, they scrutinize applicants' online personas before they even consider them for an interview. In fact, according to reports, nearly 65% of admission officers deem it fair and appropriate to review an applicant's social media presence (Expert Admissions n.d.). What they're trying to do is make sure that your online demeanor and behavior match up with their institutional values and ideals. A single questionable or controversial post has the potential to cast long shadows on an otherwise flawless application. Similarly, when you're applying for jobs, employers might conduct background checks that use your digital footprint to gauge your alignment with their company culture and values. Nothing you do online is completely private.

So, how can you proactively manage and minimize your digital footprint to maintain a cleaner, more intentional online presence? First and foremost, regularly check your social media accounts to review and update your privacy settings. Platforms like Facebook and Instagram provide extensive options for controlling who can view your posts and personal information. Update your privacy settings regularly to protect your personal space from unwanted attention. Take time to review your online presence and remove any old or irrelevant posts that do not reflect who you are today. While your digital history may not disappear entirely, taking these steps makes it much less likely that a college admissions officer will come across something that could hurt your chances.

It's also important to be aware of cookies and tracking. Cookies are small files stored on your device by websites, and they're designed to remember your preferences or login details for a smoother user experience. However, they also contribute to your digital footprint by subtly tracking your online behavior (Nguyen 2025). Browser extensions can help you manage cookies and trackers, giving you greater control over what information is collected about you. Adjusting the privacy settings on your browser can also limit the amount of data shared with websites and help you protect your digital identity.

Digital Footprint Reflection Exercise

Take a moment now to reflect on your online activities over the past month. Consider the types of content you've shared and the platforms you've engaged with most frequently. Does this compiled digital persona reflect your actual values? Would you be comfortable if prospective colleges or employers got hold of this information about you?

You can present a positive, authentic online identity by being aware of your digital actions and taking proactive steps to manage your digital footprint carefully. I know it's a bit scary, but it's really just something to be aware of so that you stay in control.

Protecting Your Personal Information Online

Nowadays, nearly every interaction and purchase happens online, so safeguarding your personal information is really important. Personal information refers to any data that identifies you. It includes your Social Security number, home address, phone number, and email address. This data holds immense value, not just for you, but for those who might misuse it. It's scary to think about someone accessing your bank account or pretending to be you online, but it does happen. Sharing sensitive information can lead to identity theft, financial loss, or unauthorized access to your accounts, and this means you should always think twice before entering your personal details on websites or sharing them on social media. Be cautious with what you share; a casual post tagging your location or showing your new ID card might seem harmless, but it can be a goldmine for cybercriminals.

Creating strong passwords is your first defense in protecting your online accounts. But how do you create one that's both strong and memorable? Start by making it long—I always go for something with at least 12 characters. Mix uppercase and lowercase letters, numbers, and symbols to make it complex, and avoid using easy-to-guess information like your birthday or simple words like "password123." I can't remember who first told me about this way to create a password, but it's by far my favorite: Think of a phrase or sentence that's meaningful to you, and use the first letter of each word, adding numbers or symbols for extra security. For example, "I love pizza on Fridays!" could become "Ilpof!2023". You can use a password manager if you have trouble remembering your passwords. Their sole purpose is to store and generate strong passwords and keep them secure and easily accessible whenever you need them, and this means you don't need to remember them.

Passwords are one layer of security, but two-factor authentication (2FA) offers you an additional layer that I always recommend. It requires two forms of verification before it will grant you access to your account—typically a password plus something else like a text message code or a fingerprint scan (Kirvan and Loshin 2024). Setting up 2FA on popular platforms is straightforward. Most services provide step-by-step instructions under their security settings, and often give you no choice but to enable it. When adding this extra layer of security means that even if someone gets your password, they cannot access your account without the second verification step. This greatly lowers the risk of unauthorized access and gives you confidence that your accounts are better protected.

You've probably heard of phishing scams. These are deceitful traps set by cybercriminals designed to trick you into revealing personal information or downloading malicious software. Phishing emails often come with urgent messages, prompting you to click a link or download an attachment. They might impersonate trusted companies, warning you of suspicious activity on your account. Look for red flags such as poorly written messages, generic greetings like

"Dear Customer," or suspicious URLs (IT Governance 2025). Always triple-check before you click any links or attachments. Instead, visit the official website directly by typing the URL into your browser. If you're still unsure, contact the company using legitimate contact information to verify the email's authenticity.

Reflect on how much personal information you share online daily. Don't just think about your social media posts; consider things like signing up for newsletters or making online purchases, too. What steps can you take today to make sure that your data remains secure?

Navigating Social Media Wisely

Most people's daily experience of social media is scrolling through random posts, but there's more to it than meets the eye. There's a sophisticated system shaping what you see, known as the social media algorithm. It's designed to present a curated flow of content seemingly tailored just for you. The social media companies analyze many data points like your past interests to make sure that your feed is an engaging space that holds your attention.

If you've found yourself immersed in the delightful antics of cat videos or engrossed in elaborate travel vlogs, it's no accident. This is a direct result of algorithmic curation, where your interactions such as clicks, likes, comments, and shares send signals to algorithms that shape what you see next. The design is intuitive, and it's always learning and adapting to your evolving interests. This can give you a comforting sense of familiarity, but it also creates a bubble that limits your exposure to new or contrasting viewpoints, and it restricts the diversity of the information you receive (Beetson 2019). This might sound like bad news, but it does not have to hold you back. Now you understand how the algorithms work, and you have the power to break free from this echo chamber by consciously searching for new content that challenges or expands your usual perspectives.

This covers what you see on social media, but what about what you do? Your social media presence is like your personal spotlight. Every post, comment, and share helps tell the world who you are, what you value, and the impact you hope to create. Whether you express yourself through thoughtful debates, creative endeavors, or inspiring anecdotes, each action you take contributes to this digital identity. The best thing you can do online is to be your authentic self. When you genuinely show up, you attract real connections and find communities that share your passions. Jump into groups or forums about things you truly care about because these are the places where meaningful conversations happen and where you can support the causes that matter to you. When you are genuine and interact with honesty, you naturally build a strong and respected reputation online.

The digital landscape, buzzing with endless notifications and perpetually updating feeds, can be overwhelming, and it's important to maintain your mental health. The allure of constant connectivity can easily become overpowering, and it can lead to a phenomenon known as "social media fatigue." You'll be able to recognize it if you notice yourself becoming less interested in social media, if you find yourself anxious and irritable about trying to keep up with it all or you have to be disconnected for a while, or if you tend to compare yourself to other people's curated lives online unfavorably (Redillas 2024).

To keep these symptoms at bay, you'll need to set healthy boundaries for yourself. For instance, you might restrict your social media to specific times of day, such as an hour in the morning and an hour in the evening. This gives you a more intentional way to manage your screen time and helps you stay present in the real world. Pay attention to signs of fatigue and when you notice them, take a step back and reconnect with offline experiences. Try to do activities away from your devices to give you a fresh perspective for your overall well-being.

It's also important to be able to discern fact from fiction. The sheer volume of content online disguises falsehoods as truths, and this means that you'll have to evaluate the credibility of all the content you consume carefully. Reliable sources, such as established news outlets and verified accounts, should be your informational anchors. Don't trust "news" you see on social media unless you're absolutely sure it's coming from a credible source. The internet is filled with misinformation, often hidden behind attention-grabbing headlines or written by authors you do not know. When I am unsure about something, I use fact-checking tools like Snopes, FactCheck.org, or even ChatGPT because they help you find out the facts. To stay credible online, always check your sources before sharing information. It's very important to protect your reputation by sharing only what you know is accurate.

Cyberbullying

Anyone who engages with online spaces, no matter their age or background, is vulnerable to cyberbullying. As I'm sure you know, this is a digital form of harassment, and the harmful behavior it encompasses is significantly amplified through the vast reach of the internet. It manifests in numerous ways, ranging from hurtful and malicious messages and spreading defamatory rumors, to posting embarrassing photos or videos without your consent (UNICEF n.d.). Unlike teasing, which might be playful and mutual, bullying involves a notable power imbalance and an intent to cause harm. It's important to recognize these behaviors as early as possible so that you can take practical steps to combat them.

Spotting the signs of cyberbullying in other people can sometimes be tricky, since it often leaves hidden scars. Still, it frequently results in victims feeling increasingly isolated, perpetually anxious, or even afraid to engage in digital interactions (Kaspersky n.d.). Recognizing these signs and understanding what they mean puts you in a great position to support your friends if you notice something is wrong. The best thing you can do is reach out to a teacher or talk to your parents about how to help.

You can also contribute to a culture that's rooted in kindness and respect. If everyone did this, cyberbullying wouldn't be so prevalent. The digital world could be a place where everyone engages with others as thoughtfully and considerately as they would in face-to-face encounters, and we can encourage this by being mindful of our own behaviors. By actively encouraging inclusive and supportive interactions, you'll help to create a culture of safe spaces where everyone feels welcome. This means being perpetually mindful of your words and actions online and encouraging others to exercise the same level of consciousness. If you witness someone being bullied, you can do something about it. Sometimes, all it takes to demonstrate that bullying will not be tolerated is to speak up or report the behavior.

If you find yourself faced with cyberbullying, remember that you're not alone. Tell your parents, a teacher, or a counselor so that you have someone in your corner from the beginning. Seeking support and advice from adults you trust is always a good idea. They can provide invaluable guidance, offer much-needed perspective, and help you navigate the situation more effectively. Next, start keeping a record of any bullying you see by taking screenshots and saving messages as evidence. Most social media platforms have simple tools for reporting bullying, so it helps to learn how these work ahead of time. That way, if something ever happens, you will know exactly how to respond.

Meanwhile, to protect yourself from the impact of cyberbullying, lean on your friends! Those people who uplift you and share your positive values. Friends are a huge source of comfort and strength during challenging times, and this will help your emotional resilience. Be mindful of how you manage your emotions online. When you encounter negativity, try simple techniques like taking a few deep breaths or stepping away from your screen to clear your mind. These small acts of self-care can make a big difference in protecting your mental well-being and remind you that who you are goes far beyond anything that happens online.

Build Your Resilience

Reflect on moments when you've faced either cyber or physical unkindness. How can you channel those pivotal experiences to build a stronger resilience? You might want to write a detailed journal entry about the insights you've gained from experiences like this and think about ways you can support others in similar situations.

Building a positive online culture starts with each of us making smart and thoughtful choices every day. The digital world plays a big role in your life, but it is important to use it safely and with intention. Still, it is just one part of your life, and you should never let it overshadow your real-world experiences. To make sure you stay balanced and fulfilled, we will look at goal setting next because this is the key to creating a life that feels truly meaningful.

CHAPTER 8

GOAL SETTING AND ACHIEVEMENT

"Setting goals is the first step in turning the invisible into the visible."

— TONY ROBBINS

Every time you're given a piece of homework, you've been set a goal: Your job is to complete that piece of work and hand it in before the deadline. But you also have the power to set your own goals, and doing this can help you achieve anything you truly want. Setting goals gives you a sense of autonomy and independence, it's a great motivator, and it makes you more likely to enjoy a task (Sutton 2024). Before we dive in, let us take some time to explore your interests so you can figure out what you truly want to work toward.

Discovering Your Passions and Interests

Have you ever been asked to write about your interests in school and realized you don't have a clue about where to start? Perhaps you have a couple of activities that you do outside of school, but are you really interested enough in them to call them a passion? You might already have an idea which makes things easier but a lot of teenagers are still figuring out what really excites them. Discovering what you love can be a fun adventure, but it does take a bit of courage. Be open to trying new things because you never know what might surprise you or light you up. Your mission is to find those activities and interests that make you lose track of time and fill you with energy and curiosity.

Let's start with what you know already. Try listing out the hobbies and activities you enjoy. It could be sketching superheroes, coding late into the night, or organizing events. Reflect on experiences you've had in the past that brought you genuine joy. Was it the thrill of scoring a goal in soccer or the contentment of baking a perfect cake? These moments offer clues to your interests, and those interests will probably be things that will motivate you throughout your entire life (Schwartz 2020). As you explore these activities, you'll start to see patterns, and you'll notice which pursuits consistently light up your spirit.

But interests alone aren't enough. It's also important to be aware of your talents and strengths. Consider what comes naturally to you. Is it problem-solving or storytelling? Maybe it's crafting or building things. If you're not sure, you can find strengths assessment tests online that will give you more insight into your abilities. A "Strengths Profile" is a good place to start. A test like this will highlight areas where you excel, and this, in turn, will help you see your potential passions. If you don't want to take a strengths test, you could try journaling about moments of personal achievement instead. Write about times when you felt proud of something you accomplished, no matter how small it was. Each thing you write about will reveal something about your strengths, and from here, you'll be able to take paths that allow you to use and develop them.

Sometimes you need to step outside your comfort zone to discover what you really love. Trying something new is always a good move. Maybe you will join a debate club, take part in a community workshop, try a new sport, or sign up for a cooking class. The point is to give yourself a chance to explore things you have not tried before—things that challenge you and open your mind. Sticking to your usual routine might feel safe but it will not show you anything new about yourself. Go after experiences that give you new perspectives and you might find passions you never knew you had.

Reflecting on your values and motivations will give you another layer of understanding. Your values will help you steer your choices toward meaningful activities. Try writing about what matters most to you. It could be anything—creativity, helping others, or learning new things, perhaps. You can talk about them with your friends, too, which may help you figure out why certain activities resonate with you more than others and help you pick new ones that excite you. This will also help you align your goals with your personal values, ultimately ensuring that every activity you pursue feels authentic to who you are.

Passion Exploration Journal

Create a journal dedicated to exploring your passions. To give you a clearer idea of what motivates you, divide it into sections: interests, strengths, new experiences, and values. Don't just do this once and forget about it, though. Reflect on each area regularly, jotting down discoveries, insights, and reflections as they come to you.

What I'd like you to remember as you're doing this exploratory work is that you're not just writing down a list of hobbies; you're figuring out what you need in your life to make it truly fulfilling. As you uncover what truly excites you, remember that it's okay if your interests evolve. In fact, you should expect them to! Life is dynamic, and so are your passions. You're not going to be one thing you're entire life: You're on a journey to self-discovery, and that's a journey that lasts as long as you do.

So why are we talking about your interests, strengths, and values in a chapter about goal setting? It's because these are the things that will enable you to set goals that resonate with who you are. You're building a foundation for meaningful goal-setting that aligns with your authentic self.

Now you're ready to start setting goals with the clarity and self-awareness you've gained, using an exciting new approach I've created specifically for you: LION goals.

Setting LION Goals

In case you haven't heard of it yet, LION stands for Legendary, Intentional, Organized, and Now-Focused. Setting goals using the LION method ensures they're inspiring, purposeful, clear, and actionable.

Let's say you want to improve your math skills. A LION goal might look like this: "I will study math for 30 minutes each weekday to raise my grade from a C to a B by the end of the semester." This goal is legendary (it pushes you toward meaningful improvement), intentional (it supports your bigger academic goals), organized (it gives a structured approach), and now-focused (it includes immediate daily actions).

First up is making your goals Legendary and Intentional. Legendary goals inspire and challenge you to strive toward something you'll be genuinely proud of achieving in the future. Intentional goals align closely with your interests and long-term vision. For instance, rather than saying, "I want to do better in school," try setting a specific and intentional goal, such as "I want to earn an A in math this semester." This gives you an exact and meaningful target. Avoid vague goals! The more precise and purposeful your goal, the more motivated you'll feel.

Next, let's focus on Organized. Goals need a plan. Break your larger goal into manageable, straightforward steps. Suppose you're passionate about music but short on time. In that case, your organized goal might involve practicing on the guitar three times per week rather than daily. Then, clearly outline your steps, prioritize them, and align them with your current situation and available resources. Being organized helps you achieve regular, small wins, which fuel your motivation and build momentum.

Lastly, your goal should be Now-Focused. Set clear timelines and deadlines to create a sense of urgency and prevent procrastination. Returning to our earlier example, setting a goal like "I will achieve an A in math by the end of the semester" clearly sets a timeframe. Use tools like calendars, reminders, or apps to keep track of deadlines, separating short-term tasks from long-term milestones. This visual structure makes big goals less overwhelming and easier to achieve.

Developing an Action Plan

Once you've defined your LION goal, develop an action plan roadmap outlining each step needed to achieve it. Break your goal down into smaller tasks and prioritize them based on their urgency and importance, as we discussed earlier.

For example, if your goal is to run a 10K in three months, begin with smaller running milestones each week. Include additional tasks, such as strength training, to build toward your overall goal gradually. If you're learning to play the guitar, break down your goal into purchasing a guitar, finding online lessons, and scheduling daily practice sessions.

Identify resources and support systems upfront. Mentors, such as teachers or older siblings, specific materials, or helpful apps, can smooth your journey. Having these in place from the start prevents unnecessary roadblocks.

Tracking Your Progress

Regularly checking your progress makes reaching your goals much easier. Set aside time each week to look at what you have accomplished and adjust your plans if needed. Progress tracking apps like ClickUp, Hive, or Habitica can give you helpful reminders and visuals of how far you have come.

Make sure to celebrate your wins along the way to keep your motivation high. Create vision boards or keep a journal where you track your achievements, the challenges you have overcome, and the lessons you have learned.

Adjust your goals and strategies regularly. Every few months, reassess and adapt your plans to fit changing circumstances or opportunities. This flexibility demonstrates growth and ensures the continued relevance and attainability of your goals.

Seek regular feedback from mentors or peers to stay encouraged and gain fresh insights that help you navigate toward success.

Goal setting with the LION method is more than just reaching your current goals. It helps you build important skills like organization, problem solving, adaptability, and time management. These abilities will support you not only with your current plans, but also as you take on bigger challenges and chase even bigger dreams in the future.

CHAPTER 9
CAREER EXPLORATION AND PLANNING

"The only way to do great work is to love what you do."

— STEVE JOBS

Now, before we get started with this chapter, I don't want you to panic. You're not supposed to have it all figured out just yet, although I'm sure it's sometimes felt like that if you've ever had a careers advisor come in to talk to your class at school. This stage of your life is all about exploring the options and thinking about what you might like to do. There is nothing wrong with changing your mind later—you might even have several different careers throughout your life. My goal is to give you a strong starting point, so you know how to approach these choices and have the skills you need to apply and interview for jobs when the time comes. It is about being prepared, not having all the answers right away.

Exploring Different Career Paths

There are so many possibilities out there. How do you know where to start? How will you figure out which path is the best match for your passions and talents? This is where understanding career clusters comes in handy. Career clusters are groups of professions that share similar skills and interests (Coursera 2025). Thinking about the clusters rather than thousands of individual jobs will make it easier for you to navigate your options. For instance, there's a cluster you can explore if you're interested in healthcare, where you might find roles ranging from nurses to lab technicians. Another cluster might focus on information technology, offering software development or cybersecurity paths. Can you see how that's a bit less intimidating than approaching each possible job individually?

Of course, even if you start this process by approaching clusters rather than specific jobs, you'll still need to have an understanding of your interests and skills. You might be a creative soul who loves to write stories or a tech enthusiast who thrives on coding challenges. Identifying these passions can be as simple as taking a skill assessment questionnaire, which will show you where your strengths lie and what careers might suit you best. High 5 Test is one you can find online for free. Interest surveys and personality tests will give you even more insights and help you uncover talents you might not realize you have (as well as confirming the ones you know about). 16 Personalities is a good one.

Once you have identified potential career paths, it is time to explore them more deeply through research. Online career exploration tools can provide detailed information about job responsibilities, required qualifications, and future growth in each field. Career Explorer is a great starting point, and many other platforms offer valuable insights to help you compare different careers and make informed decisions. Do not stop at online research. Take the next step by setting up informational interviews with professionals who work in the fields that interest you. Sitting down with someone who has real-world experience can be one of the most eye-opening parts of your journey. Their stories and advice will offer perspectives that no article or website can fully explain.

Industries evolve, and this means that it's also important to understand the trends and changes in any field you may be considering. This will help you to make well-informed decisions about your future. For example, technological advancements and healthcare research mean that the medical field is ever-evolving, and this means there are always new opportunities for people pursuing a path in the industry (Thimbleby 2013). If you want to stay up-to-date with emerging trends, reading industry publications is a good idea. You can also follow industry leaders on social media to get real-time insights into what's shaping the job market. Making use of resources like this will mean you're not just dreaming about a future career; you're preparing for it with the latest knowledge.

Career Cluster Exploration

Create a chart with major career clusters, and list at least three careers within each cluster. Note the skills each job requires, and reflect on which clusters resonate the most with your interests and abilities.

Exploring different career paths is not just about settling on a job. It is about discovering where your passions connect with professional opportunities. Whether you are drawn to the creative arts, fascinated by science, or intrigued by the world of business, there is a path for you to explore. Remember, the goal is not just to find any job but to find one that fits you well and matches your skills with your ambitions.

Building a Standout Resume

A resume is something you might need sooner than you think. We're focusing on careers in this chapter, but even if you apply for a weekend job, you might be required to submit your resume. It might seem daunting at first, but it's really just a case of creating a snapshot of who you are and what you bring to the job.

The first part is easy. You start with the basics: your contact information. Make sure that your name, phone number, and email address are easy to spot at the top. Next is the objective statement, a short sentence about your career goals and what you want to accomplish through this job (Indeed 2025). Make sure it clearly connects to the role or position you are pursuing. Then, list your education; include your school name and expected graduation date. If you already have exams that you've passed, include these too, along with your grade. Follow this with any work experience you have, even if it's volunteering, cutting grass, or babysitting. Highlight any role where you had responsibilities or learned something valuable. Finally, outline your skills, especially those that are mentioned in the job description. Skills like teamwork, problem-solving, or anything specific to the job should be included here.

When it comes to designing your resume, keep it simple. Choose a clean font, like Arial or Calibri, and stick with it throughout. Make sure you use a consistent font size for the headings and body text. A touch of color can make your resume pop, but don't go overboard—subtlety works best here, and it would be best kept to headings. White space provides breathing room for the reader's eyes, so be careful not to cram everything together or make the page look busy. You can use bullet points to make sure that none of your achievements are lost in a sea of text. You want each section to stand out and flow seamlessly into the next. You can find free downloadable resume templates online, which will help you if you're struggling with the layout.

Presentation is important for keeping the employer engaged and grabbing their attention, but it's by highlighting your achievements and skills that you can truly shine. Dynamic verbs are your friends here—words like "developed," "organized," or "led" will give life to your past roles. You want to be sure to expand on each idea, too, showing what you achieved in your role. For example, someone applying for a marketing job who had experience of using social media for marketing might say, "Managed social media platforms, increasing engagement by 30%," rather than, "Responsible for managing social media." Do you see the difference? Quantifying achievements with metrics like percentages or numbers grabs an employer's attention and provides concrete evidence of your impact (Indeed 2025). If you've won awards or received commendations, mention them. Anything that sets you apart from the crowd deserves a spotlight.

It's important that you tailor each resume for each specific job application—you can't just send out the same one every time. It is like choosing the perfect playlist for a road trip with friends. When you pick the right songs, it sets the mood and shows you care about making the experience awesome for everyone. It also means you'll be able to highlight different strengths and skills according to what most suits each role. You'll learn about these by researching the company's culture and values. Look at their website or social media to see what they believe in and represent. Use this insight to adjust your objective statement so that it's in line with their mission. If a company values innovation, highlight experiences where you've been creative. If they value initiative, flag up roles where you've had to lead or you were responsible for managing your own time. When you're applying for different roles, tweak the skills section to match the job description closely. This will show the employer that you're not just casting a wide net but genuinely interested in what they offer.

Sample Resume Templates

Check out templates that provide structure while still allowing you to customize them—websites like Canva or Microsoft Word offer versatile options that look both modern and professional.

Mastering Job Interviews

If you've done a good job with your resume, and the employer determines that you may be a good candidate for the position, you'll be called to interview. For many people, this is a nerve-wracking thirty minutes, but no matter how nervous you are, you can find the confidence you need to impress them. To walk in confidently, you're going to need to be prepared. One way to prepare is by practicing your responses to common interview questions. These typically include queries about your strengths, weaknesses, and why you're interested in the position. The STAR method—Situation, Task, Action, Result— is an excellent method to use to structure your answers. The situation is where you set the scene and give a description of the situation. For the task, you describe your responsibilities as they relate to that situation. For action, you explain what steps you took in order to achieve the task. Finally, for the result, you talk about what outcomes you achieved as a result of your action (Boogaard 2024). Following this structure will help you to articulate your experiences clearly and showcase your problem-solving skills effectively. It's a good idea to practice doing this in mock interviews with your friends or family. Not only will it build your confidence, but they'll be able to give you feedback so you can improve your responses if necessary.

Rehearsing it like this will make you feel more confident and ready to land that position!

Remember, you only get 7 seconds to make a first impression. Make it count. Show your best manners, lead with respect, and greet the world with a smile. Start each day by offering a genuine compliment or putting someone else first. The impact you make could change your day and someone else's for the better. There is no reason to wait. Start today, and let kindness and respect shine through in everything you do.

What you wear says a lot before you even utter a word. Dressing for success means making clothing choices that fit with the industry you're aiming to enter. If you're heading into a corporate job interview, a suit or a neat dress will communicate your professionalism. For a more creative field, you might opt for something casual yet polished—think smart jeans paired with a blazer, for example. Your clothes should reflect not just the role, but your confidence and readiness. Remember, it's not about being flashy but showing respect and seriousness for the opportunity. A well-chosen outfit can boost your self-assurance, too, so take the time to plan it out (Crowe Watson Recruitment n.d.).

Your secret weapon in an interview, however, is not what you wear. It's your demonstration of soft skills. Employers look for candidates who can communicate efficiently and work well in teams (Indeed 2025). Sharing examples from past experiences where you've shown leadership or solved problems collaboratively can highlight these qualities (and in Chapter 10, we'll look at some ways you can develop them). Maybe you organized a school event or led a group project to success—these are stories worth sharing.

During the interview, the active listening skills we talked about in Chapter 2 will really help you. Nod to show that you're engaged, maintain eye contact, and respond thoughtfully to what the interviewer says. This showcases your communication skills and builds rapport, making you memorable for all the right reasons (Archambeau 2023).

You might think that you're done as soon as the interview is over, but you're not finished yet. The next thing to do is follow up with a thank-you note to confirm your interest and keep yourself in the interviewer's mind. A simple email expressing gratitude for their time and excitement about the position can set you apart from candidates who don't bother with this step. Timing is essential— send your thank-you note within 24 hours to ensure that it's timely and relevant. Keep it succinct yet sincere, leaving a positive lasting impression that might tip the scales in your favor when the interviewers are making their final decisions.

Email Template for Follow-Up Notes

To make this easier for you, here's a simple template you can use for your thank-you note:

"Subject: Thank You for the Opportunity

Dear [Interviewer's Name],

Thank you for meeting with me today to discuss the [Job Title] position at [Company Name]. I am very excited about the opportunity to join your team and contribute to [mention something specific discussed during the interview].

I appreciate learning more about the innovative work at [Company Name] and am eager to contribute my skills in [mention relevant skill] to your team.

Thank you once again for this opportunity.

Best regards,
[Your Name]"

Networking for Future Opportunities

Networking is a mysterious concept to many young people, but it's really just about making connections—and I don't just mean handing out business cards or exchanging LinkedIn profiles—I'm talking about building genuine connections that can lead to exciting opportunities. Networking can open doors to internships, job offers, and even mentors who can guide you through your career path. Think about it: Many people land jobs not through online applications but through who they know. Research shows that around 80% of jobs are found through networking, which shows you how your soft skills are so important (Ton 2020)! The professional connections you make can lead you to advice and support, sometimes opening up unexpected career paths that suit your interests and skills perfectly.

You do not need to wait until you begin your career to start building your network. This is something you can begin developing right now. To get started, you need a clear strategy. Begin by identifying potential contacts such as teachers, classmates, family members, friends, or professionals in fields that interest you. Then set specific networking goals. You might want to learn more about a certain industry or ask for career guidance. Write your goals down and use them to build a networking action plan. This plan should include who you want to connect with, how often you plan to reach out, and what topics you would like to discuss. Contact management apps, such as Contact Plus, can help you organize these connections and remind you when to check-in. Staying in touch regularly shows others that you value the relationship and are serious about building meaningful connections.

Social media has made networking much easier, and you don't necessarily need to go to an event to do it. LinkedIn is a great way to connect with industry professionals. Before you do this, you'll want to optimize your profile—use a professional photo, come up with a concise headline that reflects your aspirations, and list your relevant experiences and skills. Then you can start to engage with industry groups and discussions to make your presence known. Comment on posts, share relevant articles, and write pieces about topics you're passions. This will showcase your knowledge and attract like-minded people who might end up becoming valuable contacts. Remember, social media is a two-way street; be proactive and responsive when others connect with you.

Physical networking events still take place, and although they may feel overwhelming at first, they offer great opportunities to expand your network. Career fairs, industry conferences, and school events are excellent settings for meeting professionals face-to-face. Before attending, spend some time researching the event and make a list of people you want to connect to during the event. Practice a short introduction that shares who you are and what you are excited to learn. During the event, aim to be both confident and approach-able. Wearing appropriate clothing can help you feel more prepared and self-assured. Focus on having genuine conversations, and ask thoughtful questions that encourage deeper dialogue. This kind of interaction builds stronger connections and gives you useful insights that can support your goals.

As promised, in the next chapter, we're going to look at how you can develop your leadership skills—and your newfound connections might well help you to shape your leadership style and find further opportunities for growth. Every connection you make in life can lead to personal and professional success. Isn't that a wonderful thing?

CHAPTER 10

LEADERSHIP AND INITIATIVE

"A leader is one who knows the way, goes the way, and shows the way."

— JOHN C. MAXWELL

In the last chapter, we talked about being able to showcase your leadership skills on your resume. Now it's time to talk about how you can develop them. You might think that would be something for later in life, but you can be a leader now, and you may already be without even knowing it!

Identifying Leadership Traits

My friend's son James, who I've mentioned before, is a passionate soccer player, and I've watched him play more times than I can count. Over time, I've even become familiar with his teammates. One player who always stands out is a quiet kid named Aron. He does not say much off the field, but something changes when he steps onto the field. In the most intense moments of the game, he takes charge by encouraging his teammates and giving clear and confident direction. Aron shows what it means to be a true leader. His actions reflect integrity and resilience. Integrity means staying true to your values, especially when no one is watching, and Aron lives that out in every game.

The thing about Aron is that he is also very empathetic. As you may remember this means he understands other people's feelings and perspectives and connects deeply with his teammates. All good leaders have this trait, and their resilience means they're able to bounce back from setbacks with renewed determination. A good leader is also aware of the importance of accountability—the willingness to own up to their actions and decisions. These qualities lay the foundation for effective leadership (Center for Creative Leadership 2025).

One of the greatest leaders of all time was Dr. Martin Luther King Jr. and he stands among the greatest leaders in history, embodying these very traits and leading with a vision that inspired people across the globe. Dr. King played a key role in the American civil rights movement and was instrumental in the fight to end segregation and promote equal rights for all. His leadership in organizing peaceful protests, such as the Montgomery Bus Boycott and the March on Washington, brought national attention to injustice and paved the way for new laws protecting civil rights. He delivered the iconic "I Have a Dream" speech, which continues to inspire people of all backgrounds. His example shows how true leadership, rooted in respect, kindness, and purpose, can change the world!

How do you know if you have what it takes to be a leader? These qualities aren't always so easy to spot in yourself. The best thing you can do is reflect on times when you've taken charge or supported others. Maybe you organized a study group or coordinated a community event. Maybe you're like Aron, and the sports team you're on naturally brings out your encouragement of and empathy for others. Reflective journaling can help you here. Write about your past experiences to see moments where you displayed signs of leadership.

Emotional intelligence is really important in leadership. As you hopefully remember from Chapter 2, it's that ability to recognize and understand your emotions and those of others. Leaders with high emotional intelligence navigate team dynamics smoothly, and they're able to create harmonious environments where everyone feels valued. Morgan Freeman is often noted to be a great leader, and his emotional intelligence has been pivotal to his success. He connects with people profoundly, making them feel heard and understood. His calm presence, thoughtful communication, and genuine empathy have helped him earn respect and admiration both on and off the screen.

Building confidence in your leadership abilities is essential too but remember confidence is not about being the loudest in the room. It is about trusting your decisions and standing by them. Confidence-building exercises can help—try stepping out of your comfort zone with small challenges like volunteering to lead a class project or speaking up in meetings. This will build your confidence incrementally without you needing to do anything too scary. Visualization techniques are also effective for confidence building: See yourself successfully leading a team or achieving a leadership goal. Visualizing success creates a mental blueprint that will boost your self-assurance (Segreto 2025).

The great thing about leadership is that it is not about fitting into a mold but about embracing your own unique style. You might be a collaborative leader who thrives on teamwork or a visionary who is driven by big-picture thinking. Whatever your style is, own it and keep refining it with courage. The more genuine you are, the more people will be drawn to your leadership because authenticity always stands out.

Leadership Reflection Exercise

Grab a notebook, and dedicate a section to leadership reflections. Write about times you've led or supported others—what went well? What could be improved? Reflect on how these experiences show qualities that you can develop as a leader.

Leadership is not just for adults and it is a skill you can start building now. Whether you are captaining a sports team or leading a club, there are plenty of opportunities to develop these traits and skills. Every chance you get to grow, learn, and inspire those around you will become an important part of your leadership journey.

Leading by Example

Even though James was not always confident speaking in front of a crowd, he has always had a quiet strength that everyone respects. He leads by doing—helping classmates with tough math problems, stepping up to organize community service projects, and always showing what real commitment looks like. When James takes action, people notice and want to join in because he is real and genuinely cares. He may not be the loudest person in the room, but he is always steady, honest, and true to himself. That is why I am sure he will be an awesome leader in the future.

Leaders who inspire change through their actions can create a real impact. One powerful example is Rosa Parks, a Black woman who famously refused to give up her seat on a bus to a white passenger, challenging the segregation laws of her time. Her arrest for this act sparked a movement and showed the world that one person's actions can drive big change (Burke 2023). Leading by example does not always mean standing up to huge challenges, it can be as simple as bringing good energy to group projects or helping clean up after an event without being asked. These small actions show what you stand for, encourage respect and accountability, and inspire others to step up, too!

Modeling positive behavior starts with your everyday choices. Let's say you're part of a school club and you're planning an event. You can make a huge impact by arriving early and prepared because you'll show that punctuality matters. Others will notice and do the same because they're motivated by your example. Responsibility and respect are contagious when you display them openly. A good way to make sure you do this is to come up with conduct guidelines for yourself. Write down what you value, and commit to upholding those standards every day.

Accountability is another part of leading by example—owning your actions and decisions. Let's say you're working on a group project that hits a snag because of your miscalculation. It might be tempting to deflect blame in this situation, but a better idea would be to acknowledge the mistake and suggest ways to fix it. This honesty will earn you respect and encourage others to take responsibility for their roles. You see this in sports all the time. The team captain publicly takes the heat for a lost game and explains how they could have prepared better, which not only shows good sportsmanship but also inspires the team to improve collectively.

Integrity is important in leadership, too, because it builds trust. Remember, this is about staying true to your values, even when it's tough. Let's say you're in a situation where you witness unfair treatment at school or work. This is going to challenge you. Speaking up might be difficult, but it demonstrates integrity, and it will inspire others to do the same. Group discussions on ethical dilemmas give you a chance to explore these challenges before they happen, and they might be something you want to try with your friends. You can ask each other questions like, "What would you do if a friend was cheating on a test?" or "What would you do if you knew someone had stolen from the cash register at work?" Discussions like this can be surprisingly fun, and they'll sharpen your ethical compass and prepare you for real-world situations.

Leading by example isn't always easy as it requires consistent effort and sometimes going against the grain. Every step you take that matches your values will strengthen your leadership influence. Leadership is not about grand gestures, but about everyday actions that inspire others. When you model positive behavior, show accountability, and stand by your integrity, you create a ripple effect of impact. Even if you do not always see yourself as a leader, your actions and character make you one.

Motivating Your Peers

When you figure out what inspires people, you unlock a powerful ability to spark action and help your group reach its goals. Motivation is different for everyone, and it is important to pay attention to both intrinsic and extrinsic motivators—but intrinsic motivation is where the real magic happens. Intrinsic motivation comes from within. It is when you do something because you truly enjoy it, feel curious, or take pride in what you achieve. This kind of self-driven motivation is more sustainable and leads to greater well-being and deeper engagement in whatever you are doing. Think about how it feels to solve a tough puzzle or master a new skill just for the fun of it. That is intrinsic motivation in action. While extrinsic motivators like rewards, grades, or money can push you to get things done, they often do not last as long or feel as satisfying. The best motivation comes from tapping into what genuinely excites you and makes you want to keep going. When you understand your own drives, you can use that energy to inspire your friends and help everyone get excited about working together.

Cultivating an Inclusive Environment

Creating an environment where everyone feels included and valued is key to building a motivated team. Have you ever participated in a group activity where everyone remains silent and unsure of their roles? It feels uncomfortable, and motivation disappears quickly. When that happens, you can ease the tension with a fun and energizing activity. One of my favorite choices is "two truths and a lie." In this game, each person shares two facts and one false statement about themselves, and the group tries to guess which one is not true. It helps people open up, and before long, you will hear laughter and start to feel a stronger connection among the group. Activities like this encourage teamwork, boost creativity, and remind everyone that they are an essential part of something bigger.

You'll also make the situation feel inclusive by establishing clear team goals from the beginning. This will give the group a sense of direction and purpose, and you can further boost morale by making an effort to celebrate even the most minor accomplishments. Let's say your group completes a challenging assignment. Perhaps you follow this with a celebration (a pizza party, for example). It doesn't have to be anything enormous, and it will encourage bonding, which will drive future success and inspire ongoing enthusiasm in everyone.

The Art of Effective Communication

I don't want to spend too long on effective communication because we zoned in on this in Chapter 3, but it is a powerful tool for motivating your peers. Yet again, active listening is one of the most important parts—truly absorbing what others say and responding thoughtfully. When your friend opens up about their struggles with a particular project, your role is to listen attentively before you offer advice or feedback.

If you're thinking on a bigger scale, I'd recommend reading up on motivational speeches that have marked history (you can find many online). Words have immense power, and you'll know this from any personal experiences you've had where someone's words have ignited your determination or inspired you to do something. This is why, if you're offering feedback, it's important to do so constructively. Instead of pointing out errors by saying, "You did this wrong," aim for a more guiding approach, saying something like, "Here's how we can improve." It makes a huge difference when you can steer clear of criticism and guide and nurture growth instead.

The Power of Recognition and Reward

Have you ever seen those videos where a dog is told they are a good boy or girl, and their whole face lights up? Recognition works in a similar way for people. Think about how awesome it feels when someone recognizes your effort, even when you did not ask for it. You can help create that same positive energy in any group by making recognition a regular habit. Encourage team members to give shout-outs or write simple notes of appreciation for each other's efforts. A reward does not need to be big to make a lasting impact. Try meaningful gestures like a handwritten thank you note, a "team member of the month" certificate, or a fun award like "Most Creative Problem Solver." Small acts like these can build morale, create stronger connections, and inspire kindness throughout the group.

Motivation grows strongest in a place where everyone feels noticed, valued, and appreciated. When you have this kind of environment, you are not just reaching your goals—you are actually enjoying the journey and appreciating how much you grow along the way.

Taking Initiative in Group Settings

I'm sure you know the feeling of a classroom when the deadline for a group project is looming. It often feels like there's a sense of impending chaos in the room. This is your moment to shine: It's the perfect opportunity to showcase your ability to take initiative. To recognize a moment like this you'll need to have a keen awareness of group dynamics and be attuned to the ebb and flow of productivity and morale. Pay attention to who's struggling quietly, under the radar. Can you tell which areas of the project lack direction or coordination? By volunteering for leadership roles in these moments, you have the potential to create a remarkably positive impact. You could organize the project timeline, making sure that tasks are evenly distributed and deadlines are clear. Or you could coordinate communication among team members, acting as the central hub through which ideas and updates flow. These actions will help move the project forward and show your potential as a leader. Taking initiative is not about taking over but about skillfully guiding your group toward shared success. When you step up like this, your teammates will appreciate your effort and support. Remember, real growth happens when you get comfortable being uncomfortable—so if you feel a little nervous, that is a sign you are pushing yourself and making progress.

To be able to take initiative effectively, you'll need to develop a proactive mindset. This is really about honing your ability to anticipate needs and address potential challenges proactively before they happen. To sharpen this invaluable skill, go through potential scenarios that might pose problems to the group. Envision potential obstacles that might hinder your progress, and come up with creative solutions to address them. To really develop your skills in this area, try setting personal goals that consistently push you to take initiative across a variety of contexts, whether that's leading a study group, suggesting new activities for a club, or improving existing processes. The more you do this, the more you'll develop the mindset of someone who's prepared to act, and I can guarantee that it will have a ripple effect of progress and innovation throughout your group.

It's important to make sure that taking initiative doesn't cross the line into taking control, though. You'll need to be able to balance it with collaboration if you want a harmonious and productive team environment. You want to be able to contribute your innovative ideas at the same time as valuing the contributions and insights of others. If you're part of a group tasked with organizing a school event, for example, each member of that group brings unique strengths and backgrounds to the table, and you're going to see the most success if you can pool these talents. This way, you'll cultivate a sense of mutual respect and commitment, and teamwork will be at its most effective. Luckily for you, harmonizing your personal goals with those of the team will involve skills we've already covered: maintaining open, transparent communication and actively listening to other people's perspectives.

It probably won't surprise you, at this point, to hear me talk about the value of reflection again. Learning from your leadership experiences is an important part of personal and professional growth, and when you reflect on past initiatives, you'll get a better idea of what strategies worked well and which ones need improvement. Keeping a leadership reflection journal to document recurring experiences will help you here. Note the lessons you've learned through trial and error, and share this information with your peers. This way, you'll set the stage for valuable discussions, which will give you fresh perspectives and ideas. You may have discovered that delegating tasks efficiently lightened the overall workload, for example, or that a particular communication style got you better results. Remember to understand first before being understood!

People often think that leadership is about holding formal titles or positions, but it's actually about stepping up when you're needed and empowering others. When you work on the qualities we've discussed here, you'll become a leader who naturally inspires and influences others positively.

Sometimes, taking initiative can be stressful, especially when you're new to it, so in the next chapter, we'll explore strategies for managing it and taking care of your overall mental health—another very important life skill that everyone needs.

CHAPTER 11
STRESS MANAGEMENT AND MENTAL HEALTH

"You don't have to control your thoughts. You just have to stop letting them control you."

— DAN MILLMAN

There are many adults who don't learn how to deal with stress until they're in the midst of it, and I want to arm you with the skills you need to deal with it well before then. Life is stressful, and you're probably already very aware of this with all the pressures you're under at school. In this chapter, we're going to look at how to take care of your mental health so that you have the strength and resilience to cope whenever it feels like everything is just a little too much.

Mindfulness Practices for Teens

Most people's minds are constantly switching stations, and I've no doubt that yours is often buzzing with thoughts about school, friendships, and all the other concerns that fill your life. It's easy to feel overwhelmed by the noise, and this is why we need strategies to help us stay calm and get to a place of quiet. This is where mindfulness comes in—a practice that will help you turn down the volume on your racing thoughts and tune into the present moment.

Mindfulness means paying close attention to where you are and what you are doing without letting yourself get overwhelmed by what is happening around you or lost in thoughts about the past or future. Some people think mindfulness is about stopping your thoughts, but it is really about noticing them and letting them come and go without getting caught up in them. Rooted in Buddhist traditions, mindfulness has been practiced for centuries to cultivate inner peace and focus (Selva 2017). Today, it's embraced globally for its ability to reduce stress, enhance concentration, and improve emotional regulation (Cronkleton 2022), and it's particularly beneficial for teenagers (Mandriota 2022).

One of the easiest ways to begin practicing mindfulness is through breathing exercises. A great starting point is something called balloon breathing. Imagine a balloon slowly filling with air as you breathe in and gently shrinking as you breathe out. Inhale deeply through your nose while picturing your belly expanding like a balloon. Hold your breath for a moment, then slowly exhale as you imagine the balloon deflating (O'Sullivan n.d.). This simple technique can help you feel more calm, focused, and in control. Repeat this process a few times, and you should feel the tension melt away with each breath. For moments when you need more focus and grounding, try box breathing. For this one, picture drawing a square with your breath: Inhale for four counts along one side, hold for four at the corner, and exhale for four down the other side. Keep doing this, inhaling and exhaling along the sides, and holding at the corners, until you've completed the square (O'Sullivan n.d.).

The great thing about both of these breathing techniques is that you can use them anytime, anywhere to calm your mind and body. You could even be in class—no one would have any idea you were doing it.

Breathing isn't your only route into mindfulness practice, though, and there's a lot you can do without even changing your routine. Mindful walking is one of my personal favorites. As you walk, focus on each step—feel the ground beneath your feet and the rhythm of your movements. Notice the sensation of the wind against your skin or the sound of leaves rustling nearby. As you fall into this rhythm, you should find that your stress dissipates and you become more connected to the present moment (Sutton 2020). Another easy one to try is mindful eating. What I like about both of these things is that eating and walking are things you have to do anyway, so you may as well take the opportunity and be mindful about it. Instead of rushing through your meals, savor each bite. Pay attention to the flavors, textures, and smells (Ajmera 2025). This practice will enhance your awareness and turn an everyday activity into a moment of relaxation and being in the moment.

If you'd prefer a more guided experience, there are mindfulness apps out there to help you. Using apps like Headspace and Calm will help you to explore mindfulness through guided meditations tailored to different situations—struggling with stress before an exam, for example, or longing for peace after a hectic day. They offer structured programs ranging from beginner exercises to advanced practices, so as you become more experienced, you can try new things. If you're more inclined towards reading or listening, you might want to explore books or podcasts that delve into mindfulness techniques and their benefits, which will give you information and inspiration to deepen your understanding.

Try to integrate these practices into your life gradually and make them a regular part of your routine. You don't need to use all of them if you find they don't work for you—you can pick and choose which ones you want to use. The main thing is to embrace the moments of stillness they offer and use them to keep your stress levels down.

Mindfulness Journal Prompt

If you want to see how effective mindfulness practice is for you, set up a mindfulness journal in which you can document your experiences. Write about the mindfulness exercise you tried and how it made you feel each day. Reflect on any changes you notice in your mood or stress levels over time.

Coping with Academic Pressure

School life is a lot. You've got exams looming, deadlines breathing down your neck, and the constant hum of expectations coming at you from every direction. It's no wonder that stress is familiar to so many young people. Academic stress often stems from the pressure to excel, maintain a high GPA, and balance extracurricular activities, and these stressors can take a toll on your mental well-being and performance. Stress doesn't just make you feel overwhelmed; it impacts how well you concentrate and process information (Schimelpfening 2023). When you're stressed, your mind might wander during lectures, or you might find it hard to focus when you're studying. This, obviously, affects how well you learn and retain information, and this can make academic life much harder.

To handle these demands, you will need strong time management skills, such as those covered in Chapter 4. Try organizing your workload with a study plan that breaks tasks into smaller, manageable pieces, and make sure to prioritize assignments based on due dates and importance so you do not end up rushing at the last minute. Set academic goals that fit your abilities and commitments—there is no need to be perfect in every subject. Goals that are impossible to reach can leave you feeling discouraged and stressed. Focus on steady progress and learning as much as you can along the way.

Remember how we talked about the Pomodoro Technique? This will help you to maintain focus without burning out. During your breaks, engage in activities that will help you to relax—things like stretching, listening to music, or chatting with a friend. A break is good no matter what you do, but making sure you're mindful like this will help you to keep your energy levels up and prevent you from becoming fatigued.

It can be tempting to focus only on your studies, especially during exam season, but it is important to balance schoolwork with self-care. Taking care of yourself is crucial for both your mental health and your performance. Make sure to set aside time for activities that make you happy, whether playing an instrument, drawing, or just relaxing with your favorite show. These moments help you step away from academic stress and give you a chance to reset and recharge.

Your sleep is important here too, and you'll need to make sure you have a healthy sleep routine. Prioritize getting enough rest each night, as sleep is vital for memory consolidation and cognitive function (Pacheco 2024). This means avoiding those late-night cramming sessions! If you've ever done this, you'll know that they disrupt your sleep cycle and leave you feeling groggy the next day.

It's not always easy to strike a realistic balance between schoolwork and self-care, and if you struggle with this, you might need to schedule your downtime in your calendar, just like you would for a class or an exam. This way, you'll make sure that you have moments to unwind and recharge, and it should be easier not to feel guilty about it since it's on the calendar.

Academic pressure is a genuine concern, so it is essential to take proactive steps to manage it. Keep in mind that your classmates are likely going through the same thing. Try to talk openly with each other so you can share support and encouragement with one another. If you find yourself having trouble with particular subjects, reach out to teachers, tutors, or mentors for help, that is exactly why they are there!

Building a Support System

This brings us neatly on to the next piece of the puzzle: the power of a strong support system. Having people in your corner is really important for maintaining good mental health and managing your stress levels. Your friends can give you emotional support during tough times, and they can also give you practical support when you need it—by studying with you in the build-up to an exam, for example. Your friends, family, and mentors are all important, and this will be true at every stage of your life.

I'm sure you already have friends, but in times of stress, it's the ones who are the most supportive that are going to help you the most. Supportive friends are the ones who listen without inter-rupting, validate your feelings, and stand by you, even when things get messy. They encourage you to chase dreams and pick you up when you fall. Mentors, meanwhile, are the people who can share their wisdom and experience and give you insights that help you grow. I use the word "mentor" to cover anyone in your life who fulfills this role. It could be a teacher, a tutor, or an older friend. I encourage you to have an accountability plan with your mentor because it helps you both set clear goals, stay on track, and make steady progress together.

Make sure you nurture your bond with all of these people, however that looks for you. Maybe you meet up for coffee regularly, or you have a weekly game night. Whatever it is you do, the time you spend together will help you to build trust and make memories, which, ultimately, gives you a sense of belonging and support.

It's also worth remembering that you have support resources available at school. School counselors can give you a safe space to talk about anything, from stress and academic challenges to personal issues. They're not there to judge you, so don't hesitate to chat or set a regular appointment at their office. Your school might have peer support groups too—and if it doesn't, you can create one. Joining or forming a group will give you access to a community with whom you can share your experiences and advice. You're all in the same boat, and you're facing similar challenges; this can be hugely valuable.

If you want to expand your support network even further, you might be interested in exploring online communities. Mental health forums will connect you with people who share similar struggles and give you an anonymous platform where you can exchange thoughts and find comfort in knowing that other people share your experiences. You don't have to use a community focused on mental health, though—you could choose a positive online community based around a hobby or interest you have. You can get a real sense of belonging and camaraderie in a group like this, which will boost your mood and take your mind away from the things that are stressing you out. Make sure that any online space you join is healthy and uplifting, though. You don't want to fuel your negative feelings or start comparing yourself to other people.

Identifying Your Support Circle

Take a moment now to list the people who form your support network. Who do you turn to when you're feeling down? These people could come from any of your social groups: Consider friends, family members, mentors, or online communities that provide comfort and encouragement. If you do this now, it will be much easier to figure out who to turn to when you really need support.

Invest in your bond with each of the people you identify with by being present and attentive when you're with them. Take the time to show your appreciation for them through small gestures like sending a thoughtful message or offering help when someone else is in need. Support systems are reciprocal; the more you give, the more you'll receive. Be open to new connections too—sometimes unexpected relationships become the strongest support pillars.

The last thing I'd like to remind you of here is that reaching out for help is not a sign of weakness but one of courage and strength. Never be afraid to ask for help when you need it—we all do sometimes, and it's important that we ask for it.

Recognizing When to Seek Help

There may be times, though, when your personal support systems are not enough. If your anxiety is taking over, you may need help from an outside source. Mental health struggles often manifest as changes in behavior or mood. Common signs include persistent sadness, a lack of interest in activities, and anxiety that interferes with daily life. Behavioral changes like withdrawal from friends, declining grades, or irritability can also signal distress (Solan 2024). These symptoms suggest it may be time to reach out for professional support, and the same is true if you see them in any of your friends.

There's still a lot of stigma and misconceptions around mental health issues, and this prevents a lot of people from asking for help when they need it. Many teens fear judgment or embarrassment, and a lot of them worry that asking for help is a sign of weakness. But it's not. It's a brave thing to say that you need help, and it's a strong step toward healing. We are humans with emotions and life will continually throw you curve balls unexpectedly and we need to be open about our mental health in order to protect it. Start conversations with friends or adults, you trust about how you feel. Sharing your experiences can reduce the stigma of mental health issues and encourage others to do the same. Your mental health is as important as your physical health, and it deserves to be treated as such.

It's important to make sure that you find the right mental health professional, though. You need to make sure you're getting the right support for your needs. Therapists often provide talk therapy, helping you to explore your feelings and develop coping strategies, while counselors usually focus on specific issues like school stress or family dynamics (Fagan 2023). When you are choosing a therapist, consider their specialty, experience, and approach to therapy. It is important to feel comfortable and understood by the person who will be helping you. It is completely normal to meet with a few therapists before finding the right match. Professionals are used to this process and will not be upset if you decide to work with someone else.

If you take one thing away from this chapter, let it be this: Seeking help is not an admission of defeat but an act of courage. Use the strategies we've talked about to manage your mental health yourself, but if you need it, never be afraid to ask for help—this is a step toward healing and growth. This is something we'll explore from a different angle in our final chapter, where we'll talk about how you can develop a growth mindset—and why you should.

CHAPTER 12

EMBRACING A GROWTH MINDSET

"Success is not final, failure is not fatal: It is the courage to continue that counts."

— WINSTON CHURCHILL

We're going to step away from mental health now and talk about growth in a much broader sense. Growing is something you should be doing your whole life. It's what makes life exciting, and it's what will open the doors to new opportunities and experiences. To do this, though, you're going to need to develop a growth mindset now. We talked about this in Chapter 1, but now it's time to delve a bit further.

Understanding the Growth Mindset

Let me tell you a story about James's little sister, Nicole. She's big into skating, but she's also something of a perfectionist, and this combination has been a challenge for her at times. She talked once about a moment she had in a skate park after practicing a new trick for weeks before feeling like she might be ready to take it to the park. She said that as she stood poised to take the trick, she had two impulses: one to walk away, and the other to be brave and do the trick. The thing she was struggling with was a fear of failure. She really wanted to execute the trick flawlessly, but she was almost too scared to try in case it didn't work out. She was brave, though. She did it. This is because she has a growth mindset.

Remember that the growth mindset, a term coined by esteemed psychologist Carol Dweck, refers to the idea that through dedication and effort, our abilities and intelligence can be improved and developed over time. This contrasts with a fixed mindset, which has us view our traits as immovable. If we have a fixed mindset, we believe that we're either born with a particular skill set or we're not, and there's nothing we can do about it either way (Cote 2022). For those who adopt a growth mindset, each challenge is an opportunity for enrichment and learning, but for those with a fixed mindset, these challenges might seem like threats to their intelligence and self-worth.

A growth mindset can lead you to amazing academic and personal achievements because it keeps you from giving up and pushes you to keep learning along the way. When you build this mindset, you become more resilient and give yourself the power to keep moving forward, no matter how tough the challenges may seem. Your growth mindset will give you a love for learning, and you'll be continually driven to seek new skills and acquire diverse knowledge.

How do you develop this mindset? You need to take an active approach, and self-reflection plays a significant role. One thing I enjoy doing is starting each day with a mindful reflection exercise, reflecting on the lessons I learned from the previous day. This habit keeps me focused on growing and improving, rather than chasing perfection or letting mistakes hold me back. I highly recommend making this a part of your morning routine.

When you face challenges, try to see them as chances to stretch yourself and build new skills. Did not make the team? That is okay —now you get to decide what to do next. Maybe you focus your practice on the skills that need work or increase how often you practice. Ask for feedback from people you trust; this is not criticism, but advice that can help you grow and find new ways forward. Opening yourself up to constructive feedback is how you're going to grow and develop, no matter what it is you're doing (Sirius 2023).

At the same time, you need to learn how to recognize the triggers that lead to a fixed mindset. You're most likely to see these in the form of self-defeating internal dialogues, such as "I'll never be good at this," or "I'm just not clever enough." Thoughts like this are disempowering, and they're going to stand in your way unless you actively challenge and dissect them. Reframe your internal dialogue into one that emphasizes the possibilities (Pearce 2021). For instance, you might replace "I can't do this" with "I can't do this _yet_." It's a subtle change in language, but it's powerful, and it has the potential to dramatically alter your perspective and approach. If you catch a self-defeating thought, you'll steer yourself toward a more positive and constructive mindset.

Identifying Fixed Mindset Triggers

Are there any habitual phrases you often resort to that might suggest you have a fixed mindset right now? Write them down. Now, take each phrase and rephrase it so that it gives you room for growth. If, for example, you wrote, "I'm terrible at math," next to it, you might write, "I'm actively working on improving my math skills." What you're doing here is retraining your brain and honing its ability to recognize and counteract fixed mindset inclinations.

Overcoming Limiting Beliefs

Let's look a little more closely at those limiting beliefs. Have you ever stood on stage before an audition for a play, or on the edge of a sports field ready for a try-out, only to hear that whispering doubt in your mind saying, "You're not talented enough?" Inner dialogues that say things like this are what we refer to as "limiting beliefs" (McNally 2023). These are the sneaky, negative thoughts that come from past experiences or other people's opinions, and they try to convince us that we are not capable or do not deserve to succeed—whatever success looks like in that moment. You might notice these beliefs in any area of your life, whether it is school, sports, or relationships. No matter the situation, these limiting thoughts only create barriers that hold you back.

To overcome self-doubt, you first need to recognize when and where it appears. A journal can be a powerful way to explore these moments. Write down the times when you feel self-doubt creeping in and describe your emotional reactions. Look closely to identify what might have caused those feelings. Was it a specific situation or something someone said that made you question yourself? Once you understand where the doubt began, you will be better prepared to challenge those thoughts and respond with confidence. Over time, you may start to see patterns and learn which beliefs are quietly shaping your decisions and actions.

Once you've identified your limiting beliefs, it's time to start confronting them directly. Negative self-talk can be powerful, but you have more power, and you can silence it. One of the best methods I know of is to use affirmations. If you're new to these, they're simple but powerful, positive declarations that are designed to counterbalance negativity and help you feel more self-assured (Parker Walsh 2018).

Let me give you some ideas now:

- I am capable, and I am worthy of achieving success.
- Happiness and success are mine to create and embrace.
- Self-discipline guides my actions and builds my future.
- Every challenge helps me grow stronger and wiser.
- I believe in myself and trust in my abilities.

If you want to really enhance the power of affirmations like this, say them out loud in front of a mirror. It might feel awkward at first, but doing this repetitively will embed these statements into your mind, and seeing your reflection while you're doing it will help you to see any resistance you're having and push it aside (English n.d.). Ultimately, this will help you to reshape your thought patterns.

Affirmations are just the beginning, though. Remember cognitive restructuring, the process of deliberately reevaluating and transforming negative thoughts into constructive ones (Stanborough 2023)? This is essentially what I was encouraging you to do to identify your mindset triggers. You might, for example, replace the thought, "I always mess up," with, "I learn from every experience and grow stronger." You won't see a change overnight, but if you stick with it, I know you'll start to reprogram your thinking. You'll need to keep reflecting on your thought patterns and make a conscious effort to see your past failures as learning experiences rather than evidence of your inadequacy, and this isn't always easy to do. Keep at it, though. I believe in you!

Reframing challenges in this light can completely revolutionize your outlook and turn potential setbacks into opportunities for growth, and you can practice doing this before you even have to deal with a real challenge. Engage in thought experiments where you envision both worst-case scenarios and positive outcomes for different challenges you might face with different tasks. What lessons or growth could unfold from this situation? If you reprogram your mind, you're far more likely to see the hopeful side of the challenge if it arises for real.

Cultivating positive emotions is certainly a part of confidence-building, but it's not the whole story. It's also important that you take consistent steps towards your goals. We've talked about this already, but I want you to remember the power of setting small, achievable targets rather than trying to shoot for the whole goal all at once. As we saw earlier, this will help you to build your self-esteem, especially if you celebrate each win along the way.

Dismantling limiting beliefs isn't a quick process. You'll need to be patient, committed, and compassionate toward yourself. Every setback you face is important to your journey, and the more you practice these techniques, the more confident you'll feel about tackling new challenges and pushing yourself outside of your comfort zone.

Embracing Change and Uncertainty

Change can be exciting, it can be scary, and it's an inevitable part of life. We can't avoid it, so we may as well go with the flow and open ourselves up to new experiences and possibilities. This is how we flourish, grow, and expand our horizons beyond the ordinary. You've probably studied the Renaissance period in art or history. This is a great example of the incredible things that can come from change—it was a huge period of creativity and innovation in art and science that pulled away from traditional ways of thinking. The people who embraced new ideas and methods thrived, and made huge contributions to the remarkable advancements that would come to shape the future of human civilization (Szalay and Jarus 2022).

We don't have to think as big as the Renaissance, though. Change comes at us on a much smaller scale all the time. Think about how it is every time you move schools and have to adapt to a new environment. At first, everything feels unfamiliar and every face is unknown, but over time, you get to know all the hallways and classrooms, and the strangers morph into friends, or at the very least, classmates. This is an example of a change you have no choice but to go with, and when you do, you invite unexpected pleasures and growth into your life. We have to be flexible to do this, and flexibility is something you can develop by deliberately putting yourself into new situations. It doesn't have to be huge. Maybe you take a detour on your way home and see what you discover, or perhaps you join in with a group activity that's outside of your usual preferences. By doing things like this regularly, you'll teach your brain to accept change, and this will make more significant upheavals feel less daunting (Ridgway-Taylor 2023).

You can also use scenario planning to help manage anxiety when you are facing an uncertain future. Picture yourself taking an exam where everything goes smoothly and you answer every question; then imagine the same situation, but with much more challenging questions. Consider how you would respond in both scenarios. This simple mental exercise prepares your mind for various outcomes and helps make the unknown feel less intimidating. Uncertainty can hold you back if you let it, but if you approach it with courage and curiosity, you might even start to feel excited about what is ahead.

If you notice your anxiety rising when faced with change, return to the breathing exercises we discussed in the last chapter. Imagine each breath bringing in calmness and each exhale letting go of stress. Picture yourself reaching your desired outcome as you breathe. At the same time, keep your curiosity alive so you can see change from a fresh perspective. Try exploring new activities or projects that interest you, even if they feel a little intimidating. You might pick up a new sport, learn to play an instrument, or dive into a culture you know little about. Whatever you choose, it will help expand your outlook and make it easier to approach new situations with calm and curiosity.

You'll get the most out of this action if you commit to reflecting on your experiences. Reflect on what each new situation tells you about your inner self and the world around you. This will support your growth, show you the power of perseverance, and help you build up resilience against the uncertainties that life is certain to deliver. This often involves stepping beyond your comfort zone, but the rewards are well worth it.

Turning Setbacks into Comebacks

Did you know that Michael Jordan was rejected from his varsity team because of his height and the fact that his skills weren't up to par? Many people would have given up at that point, but not Jordan. He used it as motivation to improve his skills, and he put in an incredible amount of work to improve himself (Luna 2024). He saw it as a chance to learn. Redefining failure as feedback changes everything. Each missed shot or misstep is a lesson in disguise. Analyze every setback you face with curiosity. Ask yourself, "What can I improve?" or "How can I approach this differently next time?" This is part of having a growth mindset, and it's incredibly powerful.

When you can use adversity to build your resilience, it will make you stronger and more prepared for whatever life throws your way.

Helen Keller, who became both blind and deaf at 19 months, gives us another good example. She didn't let her disabilities define her. Instead, she became an author and activist, proving that adversity can fuel greatness (Lockwood n.d.). To build your resilience, look for activities that challenge you both physically and mentally. Rock climbing, for example, requires not just strength but also focus, and it teaches you how to push through fear and fatigue. Always follow safety guidelines. You could also try chess, which builds patience and sharpens your strategic thinking. The key is to continually challenge yourself and never let a setback hinder your progress.

To do this, you need to create a comeback plan after every challenge you face. Reflect on what happened and identify the areas where things went wrong, but do so without self-judgment. Then, outline clear steps you can take to move forward and set small goals to help you improve. This may involve asking others for help, following an online tutorial, or seeking additional training. Remember how important your support system is. Surround yourself with people who believe in you and encourage you when things get tough. They can offer perspective and advice when you feel stuck, making it easier for you to stay strong and keep going after a setback.

Celebrating your growth and progress is still important when the road has been rocky—in fact, it's especially important then! It's easy to focus on your failings, but you must acknowledge how far you've come if you're to keep your motivation strong. Reflective journaling will help you here: Write about the challenges you've overcome and the skills you've gained. Recognize your perseverance by rewarding yourself, too. This will reinforce your growth mindset and keep you excited moving forward.

No setback defines you or means you have failed for good. Every challenge is just a temporary detour on your journey to success. When you put these strategies into practice, you will discover new strength within yourself and be ready for whatever comes next. This is what real growth looks like, and it will empower you for the rest of your life!

CONCLUSION

"Strive not to be a success, but rather to be of value."

— ALBERT EINSTEIN

What better way to end than with the topic of growth? Throughout this journey, we have explored life skills that will benefit you now and in the years to come. One of the most important things to remember is that life is all about continuous growth—that is where the real rewards are found. As you work on building your self-confidence, mastering emotional intelligence, and developing all the skills we have discussed, you are equipping yourself with powerful tools that will support your growth for a lifetime.

None of the skills we have discussed in this book are just concepts to understand. They are real skills—practices to build into your daily life. When you do this, you set yourself up for a successful and fulfilling future. Self-confidence does not mean you will never feel doubt. It means trusting yourself to face whatever comes, even when you are uncertain. The truth is, none of these skills will make your life completely challenge-free, but they give you the tools to turn setbacks into opportunities for growth.

One more important thing, make it a habit to write things down along your journey. The lessons, ideas, and goals you record become valuable guides and reminders. If you do not capture them in writing, they remain only dreams. Writing things down makes your growth real and helps you track just how far you have come.

All that's left for you to do now is practice them. Apply them in your daily interactions, studies, and relationships. Practice them consistently, even when it feels challenging. The more you incorporate these skills into your life, the more natural they'll become.

Most importantly, start visualizing the life you want to build—one filled with independence, confidence, and purpose. See yourself navigating the world with clarity and courage, making resilient decisions that align with your goals and the person you want to be. Your vision for the future is more powerful than you might realize. Hold it firmly, and let it guide your actions and fuel your determination.

You have the power to shape your future, and the skills you have learned here will help you build a life that matches your values and dreams. Never be afraid to dream big—go after those dreams with determination and resilience. The path ahead might have some bumps, but every step you take moves you closer to your goals. Trust the journey, believe in what is possible, and know that you will achieve extraordinary things!

REFERENCES

Ackerman, Courtney E. July 12, 2018. "What Is Self-Acceptance? 25 Exercises + Definition & Quotes." PositivePsychology.com. Accessed June 7, 2025. https://positivepsychology.com/self-acceptance/.

Ackerman, Courtney E. November 6, 2018. "What is Self-Worth & How Do We Build It?" PositivePsychology.com. Accessed June 7, 2025. https://positivepsychology.com/self-worth/.

Adams, Scarlett. April 29, 2025. "Emotional Awareness: The Key to Stronger Relationships and Well-Being." The Knowledge Academy. Accessed June 7, 2025. https://www.theknowledgeacademy.com/blog/emotional-awareness/.

Adisa, Dorcas. October 30, 2023. "Everything you need to know about social media algorithms." Sprout Social. Accessed June 7, 2025. https://sproutsocial.com/insights/social-media-algorithms/.

Allen, Sarah. n.d. "Understanding Self-Talk and Its Effects on Our Mental Health." Dr. Sarah Allen Counseling. Accessed June 7, 2025. https://drsarahallen.com/self-talk-and-its-effects-mental-health/.

Anderson, David, Matthew Stuart, Mark Abadi, and Shayanne Gal. January 5, 2019. "5 Everyday Hand Gestures That Can Get You in Serious Trouble Outside the US." Business Insider. Accessed June 7, 2025. https://www.businessinsider.com/hand-gestures-offensive-different-countries-2018-6.

Archambeau, Shellye. March 6, 2023. "How to use active listening skills in your interview." Shellye Archambeau. Accessed June 7, 2025. https://www.shellye.opengrowth.com/article/how-to-use-active-listening-skills-in-your-interview.

Aviles, David A. July 2, 2024. "The Power of Essential Life Skills: The Most Undervalued Career Catalysts." LinkedIn. Accessed June 7, 2025. https://www.linkedin.com/pulse/power-life-skills-most-undervalued-career-catalysts-aviles-mba-mcc-vyzne.

Ayoola, Elizabeth. n.d. "50/30/20 Budget Calculator." NerdWallet. Accessed June 7, 2025. https://www.nerdwallet.com/article/finance/nerdwallet-budget-calculator.

Bambino, Samantha. July 2, 2024. "The 24-Hour Rule Is The Money-Saving Hack You Need." Money Digest. Accessed June 7, 2025. https://www.moneydigest.com/1611477/24-hour-rule-money-saving-hack-save-wait-think/.

Beetson, Heidi. November 11, 2019. "How algorithms may be reinforcing our online filter bubble." Medium. Accessed June 7, 2025. https://medium.com/@HeidiBeetson/how-algorithms-are-reinforcing-our-online-filter-bubble-53b8c06a9830.

Behal, Garima. May 5, 2025. "10 Best Goal Tracking Apps for 2025 (Free & Paid)." ClickUp. Accessed June 7, 2025. https://clickup.com/blog/goal-tracking-apps/.

Bjarnadottir, Adda, and Rachael Ajmera. March 25, 2025. "Mindful Eating 101 — A Beginner's Guide." Healthline. Accessed June 7, 2025. https://www.healthline.com/nutrition/mindful-eating-guide.

Boogaard, Kat. December 26, 2023. "How to Write SMART Goals (with Examples)." Atlassian. Accessed June 7, 2025. https://www.atlassian.com/blog/productivity/how-to-write-smart-goals.

Boogaard, Kat. May 14, 2024. "STAR Method: How to Use This Technique to Ace Your Next Job Interview." The Muse. Accessed June 7, 2025. https://www.themuse.com/advice/star-interview-method.

Britten, Rhonda. n.d. "How to Trust Yourself and Build True Self-Confidence." Fearless Living. Accessed June 7, 2025. https://fearlessliving.org/how-to-trust-yourself-and-build-true-self-confidence/.

Burke, Myles. November 29, 2023. "Rosa Parks: The 'no' That Sparked the Civil Rights Movement." BBC. Accessed June 7, 2025. https://www.bbc.com/culture/article/20231128-rosa-parks-the-one-moment-that-sparked-the-civil-rights-movement.

Chastain, Ann. December 2, 2013. "Use Active Listening Skills to Effectively Deal with Conflict." MSU Extension. Accessed June 7, 2025. https://www.canr.msu.edu/news/use_active_listening_skills_to_effectively_deal_with_conflict.

Cherry, Kendra. May 3, 2023. "Intrinsic Motivation: How Internal Rewards Drive Behavior." Verywell Mind. Accessed June 7, 2025. https://www.verywellmind.com/what-is-intrinsic-motivation-2795385.

Cherry, Kendra. January 30, 2025. "Understanding Body Language and Facial Expressions." Verywell Mind. Accessed June 7, 2025. https://www.verywellmind.com/understand-body-language-and-facial-expressions-4147228.

Cherry, Kendra. July 3, 2024. "What Is Empathy?" Verywell Mind. Accessed June 7, 2025. https://www.verywellmind.com/what-is-empathy-2795562.

Cherry, Kendra. August 9, 2024. "What Is Extrinsic Motivation?" Verywell Mind. Accessed June 7, 2025. https://www.verywellmind.com/what-is-extrinsic-motivation-2795164.

Cherry, Kendra. July 7, 2024. "What Is Procrastination?" Verywell Mind. Accessed June 7, 2025. https://www.verywellmind.com/the-psychology-of-procrastination-2795944.

Cherry, Kendra. January 31, 2024. "You Can Increase Your Emotional Intelligence in 3 Simple Steps—Here's How." Verywell Mind. Accessed June 7, 2025. https://www.verywellmind.com/what-is-emotional-intelligence-2795423.

Clancy, Marc. May 17, 2025. "How to Make an Inspiring Vision Board in Minutes with Milanote." Milanote. Accessed June 7, 2025. https://milanote.com/guide/vision-board.

Cooks-Campbell, Allaya. July 20, 2022. "Tired of playing it safe? Learn how to take risks that pay off." BetterUp. Accessed June 7, 2025. https://www.betterup.com/blog/how-to-take-risks.

Cornell, Dave. January 3, 2024. "Internal Validation: Definition and 10 Examples 2025." Helpful Professor. Accessed June 7, 2025. https://helpfulprofessor.com/internal-validation/.

Cote, Catherine. March 10, 2022. "Growth Mindset Vs. Fixed Mindset: What's the Difference?" Harvard Business School. Accessed June 7, 2025. https://online.hbs.edu/blog/post/growth-mindset-vs-fixed-mindset.

"Credit: What It Is and How It Works." October 1, 2024. Investopedia. Accessed June 7, 2025. https://www.investopedia.com/terms/c/credit.asp.

Cronkleton, Emily. February 25, 2022. "Mindfulness and emotional well-being strategies." Medical News Today. Accessed June 7, 2025. https://www.medicalnewstoday.com/articles/mindfulness-for-mental-wellbeing.

Cuncic, Arlin. February 12, 2024. "7 Active Listening Techniques to Practice in Your Daily Conversations." Verywell Mind. Accessed June 7, 2025. https://www.verywellmind.com/what-is-active-listening-3024343.

"Cyberbullying: What is it and how to stop it." n.d. UNICEF. n.d. https://www.unicef.org/stories/how-to-stop-cyberbullying.

Degges-White, Suzanne. September 24, 2018. "6 Rules for Healthy Friendships." Psychology Today. Accessed June 7, 2025. https://www.psychologytoday.com/gb/blog/lifetime-connections/201809/6-rules-healthy-friendships.

"Dressing for Success: Mastering Job Interviews with Assurance." n.d. Crowe Watson Recruitment. Accessed June 7, 2025. https://crowewatson.co.uk/dressing-for-success-mastering-job-interviews-with-assurance/.

English, Nichola. n.d. "Mastering Mirror Work for Self-Love." The Female CEO. Accessed June 7, 2025. https://www.thefemaleceo.com/blog/mastering-mirror-work-for-self-love.

Fagan, Abigail. April 12, 2023. "Psychologist Vs Therapist Vs Counselor: What Are the Differences?" Psychology Today. Accessed June 7, 2025. https://www.psychologytoday.com/gb/basics/therapy/psychologist-vs-therapist-vs-counselor.

Fernando, Jason. February 28, 2024. "The Power of Compound Interest: Calculations and Examples." Investopedia. Accessed June 7, 2025. https://www.investopedia.com/terms/c/compoundinterest.asp.

"51 Examples of General Resume Objective Statements." February 19, 2025. Indeed. Accessed June 7, 2025. https://www.indeed.com/career-advice/resumes-cover-letters/general-resume-objectives-statements.

Fiorelli, Paul E. February 23, 2023. "Integrity Builds Trust: What? So What? and Now What?" Institute of Business Ethics - IBE. Accessed June 7, 2025. https://www.ibe.org.uk/resource/integrity-builds-trust-what-so-what-and-now-what-blog.html.

Francis, Charles A. April 12, 2020. "Raise Your Emotional Awareness for More Peace and Happiness." The Mindfulness Meditation Institute. Accessed June 7, 2025. https://mindfulnessmeditationinstitute.org/2020/04/12/raise-your-emotional-awareness-for-more-peace-and-happiness/.

Globokar, Lidija. March 5, 2020. "The Power Of Visualization And How To Use It." Forbes. Accessed June 7, 2025. https://www.forbes.com/sites/lidijaglobokar/2020/03/05/the-power-of-visualization-and-how-to-use-it/.

Gordon, Ross. March 29, 2019. "Why Do I Have Conflict with Certain Friends?" Gridology. Accessed June 7, 2025. https://www.gridology.co/p/gridology-2-why-do-i-have-conflict.

Hall, Dana. n.d. "JK Rowling Turned Down By 12 Publishers Before Finding Success With Harry Potter Books." RiseUpEight.org. Accessed June 7, 2025. https://riseupeight.org/jk-rowling-harry-potter-books/.

Hancock, Jonathan. n.d. "Six Thinking Hats." Mind Tools. Accessed June 7, 2025. https://www.mindtools.com/ajlpp1e/six-thinking-hats.

Harris, Laura. March 17, 2023. "Self-worth vs. self-esteem: What's the difference?" Thriveworks. Accessed June 7, 2025. https://thriveworks.com/help-with/self-improvement/self-worth-vs-self-esteem/.

Harvey, Russell. n.d. "Psychological Safety: Why Making Mistakes is Good!" The Resilience Coach. Accessed June 7, 2025. https://www.theresiliencecoach.co.uk/blog/psychological-safety-why-making-mistakes-is-good.

Herrity, Jennifer. March 12, 2025. "How To Practice Reflective Listening (With Tips and Examples)." Indeed. Accessed June 7, 2025. https://www.indeed.com/career-advice/career-development/reflective-listening.

Hope-Jones, Eleanor. April 12, 2023. "The 5 types of accountability partner you need in your life right now." Flown. Accessed June 7, 2025. https://flown.com/blog/procrastination/the-five-types-of-accountability-partner-you-need-in-your-life-right-now.

"How to Handle Conflict with Friends." n.d. Army Cadets. Accessed June 7, 2025. https://armycadets.com/features/how-to-handle-conflict-with-friends/.

"How To Make a Comprehensive Resume (With Examples)." February 19, 2025. Indeed. Accessed June 7, 2025. https://www.indeed.com/career-advice/resumes-cover-letters/how-to-make-a-resume-with-examples.

"How To Measure Your Progress Effectively in 5 Steps." February 20, 2025. Indeed. Accessed June 7, 2025. https://www.indeed.com/career-advice/career-development/measure-progress.

"How to Spot a Phishing Email in 2025 –with Real Examples and Red Flags." May 16, 2025. IT Governance. Accessed June 7, 2025. https://www.itgovernance.co.uk/blog/5-ways-to-detect-a-phishing-email.

"Importance of Thomas Edison's Quotes." n.d. Thomas Edison Foundations. Accessed June 7, 2025. https://www.thomasedison.org/edison-quotes.

Jaworski, Bartosz. January 30, 2024. "A Guide to Conducting a Post-mortem Analysis." LogRocket Blog. Accessed June 7, 2025. https://blog.logrocket.com/product-management/post-mortem-analysis/.

Joshi, Priyankaa. n.d. "Psychology of saying sorry: why are we so bad at apologising?" Stylist. Accessed June 7, 2025. https://www.stylist.co.uk/life/sorry-apologise-hard-psychology-relationships/584667.

Kirvan, Paul. October 28, 2024. "What is Two-Factor Authentication (2FA) and How Does It Work?" Informa. Accessed June 7, 2025. https://www.techtarget.com/searchsecurity/definition/two-factor-authentication.

Krockow, Eva M. September 27, 2018. "How Many Decisions Do We Make Each Day?" Psychology Today. Accessed June 7, 2025. https://www.psychologytoday.com/gb/blog/stretching-theory/201809/how-many-decisions-do-we-make-each-day.

Landers, Bryce. August 2, 2023. "You Are What You Consume: Impact of Food, Media, and Self-Talk." Sport Speed Lab. Accessed June 7, 2025. https://sportspeedlab.com/you-are-what-you-consume-impact-of-food-media-and-self-talk/.

Lockwood, Rick. n.d. "Helen Keller." Bin Day Blues. Accessed June 7, 2025. https://www.bindayblues.com/resources/resource-helen-keller.

"Long Term Vs Short Term Savings and Investments." n.d. FNB. Accessed June 7, 2025. https://www.online.fnbci.co.uk/blog/investments/articles/LongTermShortTerm_sav_invest/.

Loria, Kevin. August 28, 2016. "There's One Thing You Can Do to Make Your Scariest Moments More Bearable, According to Psychologists." Business Insider. Accessed June 7, 2025. https://www.businessinsider.com/mental-rehearsal-psychology-strategy-anxiety-fear-2016-8.

Luna, Wilson. November 8, 2024. "Michael Jordan's Story: From High School Rejection to Basketball Legend." LinkedIn. Accessed June 7, 2025. https://www.linkedin.com/pulse/michael-jordans-story-from-high-school-rejection-basketball-luna-dravf.

MacArthur, Heather V. July 31, 2024. "Listening To Build Trust & Build Relationships." Forbes. Accessed June 7, 2025. https://www.forbes.com/sites/hvmacarthur/2024/07/31/listening-to-build-trust--build-relationships/.

Mahnot, Surbhi. March 25, 2025. "What Makes Oprah Winfrey a Great Leader? Emotional Intelligence." LinkedIn. Accessed June 7, 2025. https://www.linkedin.com/pulse/what-makes-oprah-winfrey-great-leader-emotional-surbhi-mahnot-

1lkzc.

Mandriota, Morgan. June 30, 2022. "7 Mindfulness Exercises for Teens and Tips to Get Started." Psych Central. Accessed June 7, 2025. https://psychcentral.com/health/the-benefits-of-mindfulness-meditation-for-teens.

Marr, Bernard. August 5, 2022. "13 Easy Steps To Improve Your Critical Thinking Skills." Forbes. Accessed June 7, 2025. https://www.forbes.com/sites/bernard marr/2022/08/05/13-easy-steps-to-improve-your-critical-thinking-skills/.

Martins, Julia. January 12, 2025. "7 quick and easy steps to creating a decision matrix, with examples." Asana. Accessed June 7, 2025. https://asana.com/resources/decision-matrix-examples.

Martins, Julia. August 30, 2024. "How to build your critical thinking skills in 7 steps (with examples)." Asana. Accessed June 7, 2025. https://asana.com/resources/critical-thinking-skills.

Martins, Julia. February 3, 2025. "What are SMART goals? Examples and templates." Asana. Accessed June 7, 2025. https://asana.com/resources/smart-goals.

Maxabella, Bron. April 14, 2022. "Delayed Gratification is a Key to Wealth (if You Can Wait Long Enough)." Money Wise. Accessed June 7, 2025. https://www.moneywiseglobal.com/article/delayed-gratification-is-a-key-to-wealth-if-you-can-wait-long-enough/.

McKelvie, Callum, and Elizabeth Peterson. November 2, 2022. "Who Invented the Light Bulb?" Livescience.com. Accessed June 7, 2025. https://www.livescience.com/43424-who-invented-the-light-bulb.html.

McMullen, Laura. May 30, 2025. "The 8 Best Budget Apps for 2025." NerdWallet. Accessed June 7, 2025. https://www.nerdwallet.com/article/finance/best-budget-apps.

McNally, Melanie A. June 12, 2024. "From Small Steps to Big Wins: The Importance of Celebrating." Psychology Today. Accessed June 7, 2025. https://www.psychol ogytoday.com/gb/blog/empower-your-mind/202406/from-small-steps-to-big-wins-the-importance-of-celebrating.

McNally, Melanie A. November 22, 2023. "Overcoming Self-Limiting Beliefs." Psychology Today. Accessed June 7, 2025. https://www.psychologytoday.com/gb/blog/empower-your-mind/202311/overcoming-self-limiting-beliefs.

Nash, Jo. January 5, 2018. "How to Set Healthy Boundaries & Build Positive Relationships." PositivePsychology.com. Accessed June 7, 2025. https://posi tivepsychology.com/great-self-care-setting-healthy-boundaries/.

Neff, Kristin, and Christopher Germer. January 29, 2019. "The Transformative Effects of Mindful Self-Compassion." Mindful. Accessed June 7, 2025. https://www.mindful.org/the-transformative-effects-of-mindful-self-compassion/.

Nguyen, Sara J. "What Are Internet Cookies and How Are They Used?" April 23,

2025. All About Cookies. Accessed June 7, 2025. https://allaboutcookies.org/what-is-a-cookie.

Nunez, Kirsten. August 10, 2020. "The Benefits of Progressive Muscle Relaxation and How to Do It." Healthline. Accessed June 7, 2025. https://www.healthline.com/health/progressive-muscle-relaxation.

O'Sullivan, Kelly. n.d. "3 Breathing Techniques That Actually Work." MyWellbeing. Accessed June 7, 2025. https://mywellbeing.com/ask-a-therapist/3-breathing-techniques-that-actually-work.

Pacheco, Danielle. May 9, 2024. "How Memory and Sleep Are Connected." Sleep Foundation. Accessed June 7, 2025. https://www.sleepfoundation.org/how-sleep-works/memory-and-sleep.

Page, Oliver. November 4, 2020. "How to Leave Your Comfort Zone and Enter Your 'Growth Zone'." PositivePsychology.com. Accessed June 7, 2025. https://positivepsychology.com/comfort-zone/.

Parker Walsh, Carol. December 5, 2018. "Affirmation: I Am Free of Limiting Beliefs." Parker Walsh Consulting. Accessed June 7, 2025. https://www.carolparkerwalsh.com/blog/affirmation-i-am-free-of-limiting-beliefs.

Pavlou, Marie. April 1, 2024. "The Power of Self-Reflection for Success." Medium. Accessed June 7, 2025. https://mariepavlou.medium.com/the-power-of-self-reflection-for-success-fe3774280fd1.

Pearce, Andrea. August 19, 2021. "Reframing Self-Limiting Beliefs." The Open University. Accessed June 7, 2025. https://www.open.edu/openlearn/health-sports-psychology/psychology/reframing-self-limiting-beliefs.

Perry, Elizabeth. August 23, 2022. "Breaks for breakthroughs: The importance of taking breaks during the workday." BetterUp. Accessed June 7, 2025. https://www.betterup.com/blog/the-importance-of-taking-breaks.

Perry, Elizabeth. May 15, 2023. "What Is Networking and Why Is It So Important?" BetterUp. Accessed June 7, 2025. https://www.betterup.com/blog/networking.

Phillimore, Simon. May 7, 2024. "Failure is an Opportunity for Growth and Learning." LinkedIn. Accessed June 7, 2025. https://www.linkedin.com/pulse/failure-opportunity-growth-learning-simon-phillimore-ba-hons--2f1ie.

Poyner, Nefertiti. September 3, 2024. "10 Reasons Why We Want to Start the School Year Helping Our Children Build a Strong Emotional Vocabulary." Devereux. Accessed June 7, 2025. https://centerforresilientchildren.org/emotional-vocabulary/.

Price, Emily. August 29, 2017. "Combat Procrastination by Visualizing Your Future Self." Lifehacker. Accessed June 7, 2025. https://lifehacker.com/combat-procrastination-by-visualizing-your-future-self-1797979592.

Redillas, Maria. February 22, 2024. "Social Media Fatigue: Signs, Symptoms, and How to Overcome It." Medium. Accessed June 7, 2025. https://medium.com/@

mariaisquixotic/social-media-fatigue-signs-symptoms-and-how-to-overcome-it-4e91eb80a642.

Reflections, Daily. March 5, 2023. "I Have Not Failed. I've Just Found 10,000 Ways That Won't Work."-Thomas Edison." Medium. Accessed June 7, 2025. https://medium.com/@officialprpatel002/i-have-not-failed-ive-just-found-10-000-ways-that-won-t-work-thomas-edison-6d12b1650d4b.

Richards, Louisa. March 18, 2022. "What is positive self-talk?" Medical News Today. Accessed June 7, 2025. https://www.medicalnewstoday.com/articles/positive-self-talk.

Ridgway-Taylor, Kat. December 11, 2023. "Navigating Transitions: Preparing for Big Life Changes (Including Starting a 'Boundless Life')." Boundless Life. Accessed June 7, 2025. https://www.boundless.life/blog/navigating-transitions-preparing-for-big-life-changes-including-starting-a-boundless-life.

Rios, Peggy. November 22, 2024. "How to Deal With Peer Pressure." WikiHow. Accessed June 7, 2025. https://www.wikihow.com/Deal-With-Peer-Pressure.

Robbins, Tony. n.d. "How to use 'I-statements." Official Website of Tony Robbins. Accessed June 7, 2025. https://www.tonyrobbins.com/blog/words-matter-you-vs-i?srsltid

Ronin, Kara. March 2, 2015. "How to Not Waste the First 7 Seconds of a First Impression." Executive Impressions. Accessed June 7, 2025. https://www.executive-impressions.com/blog/not-waste-7-seconds-first-impression.

Saunders, Elizabeth G. July 5, 2019. "6 Causes of Burnout, and How to Avoid Them." Harvard Business Review. Accessed June 7, 2025. https://hbr.org/2019/07/6-causes-of-burnout-and-how-to-avoid-them.

Schimelpfening, Nancy. March 13, 2023. "Stress Can Affect Your Ability to Think Clearly, Study Finds." Healthline. Accessed June 7, 2025. https://www.healthline.com/health-news/why-it-may-be-harder-to-make-good-decisions-when-your-stressed.

Schmitz, Mike. September 17, 2015. "How Martin Luther King Jr. Succeeded with Soft Skills." Conover. Accessed June 7, 2025. https://www.conovercompany.com/how-martin-luther-king-jr-succeeded-with-soft-skills/.

Schwartz, David. January 25, 2020. "Childhood Passions Can Have Long-Lasting Benefits." Psychology Today. Accessed June 7, 2025. https://www.psychologytoday.com/us/blog/adolescents-explained/202001/childhood-passions-can-have-long-lasting-benefits.

Scott, Elizabeth. December 4, 2023. "Aggressive Communication: Examples and How to Handle It." Verywell Mind. Accessed June 7, 2025. https://www.verywellmind.com/what-is-aggressiveness-aggressiveness-in-communication-3145097.

Scott, Elizabeth. April 9, 2025. "Can Mindfulness Relieve More Than Stress?"

Verywell Mind. Accessed June 7, 2025. https://www.verywellmind.com/mindful ness-the-health-and-stress-relief-benefits-3145189.

Scott, Elizabeth. September 26, 2023. "How to Use Assertive Communication." Verywell Mind. Accessed June 7, 2025. https://www.verywellmind.com/learn-assertive-communication-in-five-simple-steps-3144969.

Scott, Elizabeth. November 3, 2023. "What to Know If You're Concerned About a Toxic Relationship." Verywell Mind. Accessed June 7, 2025. https://www.very wellmind.com/toxic-relationships-4174665.

Scott, Ellen. n.d. "One Good Thing: why setting small, achievable goals is the best way to tackle overwhelm and be more productive." Stylist. Accessed June 7, 2025. https://www.stylist.co.uk/health/mental-health/small-achievable-goals/931744.

Scroggs, Laura. n.d. "The Eisenhower Matrix." Todoist. Accessed June 7, 2025. https://www.todoist.com/productivity-methods/eisenhower-matrix.

Scroggs, Laura. n.d. "The Pomodoro Technique." Todoist. Accessed June 7, 2025. https://www.todoist.com/productivity-methods/pomodoro-technique.

Segal, Troy. May 27, 2025. "What Is a Secured Credit Card? How It Works and Benefits." Investopedia. Accessed June 7, 2025. https://www.investopedia.com/terms/s/securedcard.asp.

Segreto, Paul. February 28, 2025. "Visualizing Success: A Mental Blueprint for Achievement." Medium. Accessed June 7, 2025. https://paulsegreto.medium.com/visualizing-success-a-mental-blueprint-for-achievement-1006e9960207.

Sehgal, Sanjay. July 25, 2023. "Why Emotional Intelligence Is Crucial For Effective Leadership." Forbes. Accessed June 7, 2025. https://www.forbes.com/councils/forbesbusinesscouncil/2023/07/25/why-emotional-intelligence-is-crucial-for-effective-leadership/.

Selva, Joaquín. March 13, 2017. "The History and Origins of Mindfulness." Positive-Psychology.com. Accessed June 7, 2025. https://positivepsychology.com/history-of-mindfulness/.

Shatz, Itamar. n.d. "Famous Procrastinators." Solving Procrastination. Accessed June 7, 2025. https://solvingprocrastination.com/famous-procrastinators/.

Sinusoid, Darya. December 10, 2021. "How to Anticipate the Obstacles to Achieving Your Goals." Shortform. Accessed June 7, 2025. https://www.short form.com/blog/obstacles-to-achieving-goals/.

Sirius, Mike. March 27, 2023. "The Importance of Feedback for Personal and Professional Growth." Medium. Accessed June 7, 2025. https://msirius.medium.com/the-importance-of-feedback-for-personal-and-professional-growth-a152d b826c65.

"Social Media's Impact on College Admissions." n.d. Expert Admissions. Accessed June 7, 2025. https://expertadmissions.com/social-medias-impact-on-college-admissions/.

Solan, Matthew. April 1, 2024. "How to Recognize the Signs of Mental Health Issues." Harvard Health. Accessed June 7, 2025. https://www.health.harvard.edu/mind-and-mood/how-to-recognize-the-signs-of-mental-health-issues.

Stanborough, Rebecca J. June 5, 2023. "How to Change Negative Thinking with Cognitive Restructuring." Healthline. Accessed June 7, 2025. https://www.healthline.com/health/cognitive-restructuring.

"The Story of a Man Who Was Fired for a Lack of Creativity but Went on to Build His Own Empire." n.d. Bright Side. Accessed June 7, 2025. https://brightside.me/articles/the-story-of-a-man-who-was-fired-for-a-lack-of-creativity-but-went-on-to-build-his-own-empire-798520/.

Sundström, Malin, Jenny Balkow, Jonas Florhed, and Matilda Tjernström. "Impulsive Buying Behaviour: The Role of Feelings When Shopping for Online Fashion." July 2013. ResearchGate. Accessed June 7, 2025. https://www.researchgate.net/publication/274376735_Impulsive_Buying_Behaviour_The_Role_of_Feelings_When_Shopping_for_Online_Fashion.

Sutton, Jeremy. July 15, 2020. "Mindful Walking & Walking Meditation: A Restorative Practice." PositivePsychology.com. Accessed June 7, 2025. https://positivepsychology.com/mindful-walking/.

Sutton, Jeremy. December 12, 2024. "The Importance, Benefits, and Value of Goal Setting." PositivePsychology.com. Accessed June 7, 2025. https://positivepsychology.com/benefits-goal-setting/.

Szalay, Jessie, and Owen Jarus. January 11, 2022. "The Renaissance: The 'Rebirth' of Science & Culture." Livescience.com. Accessed June 7, 2025. https://www.livescience.com/55230-renaissance.html.

"10 valuable soft skills that you need to succeed in your career." March 20, 2025. Indeed. Accessed June 7, 2025. https://uk.indeed.com/career-advice/career-development/soft-skills.

Thimbleby, Harold. "Technology and the Future of Healthcare." *J Public Health Res* 2, no. 3 (December 2013). https://pmc.ncbi.nlm.nih.gov/articles/PMC4147743/.

Thomas, Emily. n.d. "Goal-Setting Rewards That Aren't Food or Money." Cultivate. Accessed June 7, 2025. https://cultivatewhatmatters.com/blogs/cwm/goal-setting-rewards-that-arent-money-or-food?srsltid

Ton, Jeffrey. October 15, 2020. "Networking: It's Not What You Think." Forbes. Accessed June 7, 2025. https://www.forbes.com/councils/forbestechcouncil/2020/10/15/networking-its-not-what-you-think/.

Toneva, Michaela. n.d. "Unlock the Power of 5 Whys: Root Cause Analysis Made Easy." Businessmap. Accessed June 7, 2025. https://businessmap.io/lean-management/improvement/5-whys-analysis-tool.

"12 Essential Qualities of Effective Leadership." March 3, 2025. Center for Creative

Leadership. Accessed June 7, 2025. https://www.ccl.org/articles/leading-effec tively-articles/characteristics-good-leader/.

Walker, Chris M. n.d. "Chris M. Walker's Post." LinkedIn. Accessed June 7, 2025. https://www.linkedin.com/posts/superstarseo_steve-jobs-was-fired-from-applethe-company-activity-7264643584291737600-ltvm.

Waugh, Evelyn. February 2, 2024. "Authorized User Vs. Cosigner: What Is the Difference?" Experian. Accessed June 7, 2025. https://www.experian.com/blogs/ask-experian/what-is-the-difference-between-an-authorized-user-and-a-cosigner/.

West, Mary. April 21, 2022. "What to know about guided imagery." Medical News Today. Accessed June 7, 2025. https://www.medicalnewstoday.com/articles/guided-imagery.

"What Are Digital Footprints?" n.d. BBC Bitesize. Accessed June 7, 2025. https://www.bbc.co.uk/bitesize/articles/z8kdqfr#zggckty.

"What Are the Effects of Cyberbullying?" n.d. Kaspersky. Accessed June 7, 2025. https://www.kaspersky.com/resource-center/preemptive-safety/cyberbullying-effects.

"What Is a Career Cluster? 14 Types To Know." March 25, 2025. Coursera. Accessed June 7, 2025. https://www.coursera.org/articles/what-is-a-career-cluster.

"What Is a Credit Score?" May 7, 2025. Investopedia. Accessed June 7, 2025. https://www.investopedia.com/terms/c/credit_score.asp.

Wisner, Wendy. June 21, 2024. "25 Positive Daily Affirmations for Your Mental Health." Verywell Mind. Accessed June 7, 2025. https://www.verywellmind.com/positive-daily-affirmations-7097067.

Wooll, Maggie. July 30, 2022. "Master the art of learning to live with your stressors." BetterUp. Last modified July 30, 2022. https://www.betterup.com/blog/what-are-stressors.

Yeung, Anthony J. September 12, 2021. "How to Finally Beat Procrastination." Medium. Accessed June 7, 2025. https://medium.com/mind-cafe/how-to-finally-beat-procrastination-8d86382cdfaa.

www.ingramcontent.com/pod-product-compliance
Lightning Source LLC
Chambersburg PA
CBHW052115030426
42335CB00025B/2989